This Book Provides:

- Transmutation tools for a sustained and consistent Inner Peace Journey
- Practical exercises and advice for developing your intuition
- Practical methods for pineal gland detoxification
- The Remen $\bar{Q}$ process – an easy method of shifting non-peace to peace
- Remen $\bar{Q}$ Session examples
- An explanation of the third eye chakra's* role in our intuition and wellness
- An exploration of the stages of intuition development and the emotional patterns that can cause you to get stuck
- An exploration of a wounded empath and the wounded intuitive and related emotional states
- A physiological description of the pineal gland
- A deep dive into the limiting patterns known as Emotional Pathophysiology (See the Glossary)
- An exploration of the emotional states of diseases of the pineal gland and diseases associated with low melatonin levels, i.e., pineal gland impairment
- Resources for facilitating your Inner Peace Journey

*See Glossary page 116 for more information.

Alchemy of the Third Eye and Pineal Gland

Alchemy of the Third Eye and Pineal Gland

Healing Your Intuition

Valeria J. Moore

Copyright 2024 Valeria J. Moore

All rights reserved. Please get in touch with Valeria at mail@peacealchemist.com if you wish to reproduce any material in this book.

Artificial intelligence harvesting or use by artificial intelligence is not permitted.

ISBN: 978-1-7371275-5-0

Published by Three Moons Publishing
Interior design by Valeria Moore
Edited by Barbara Millikan
Cover by Valeria Moore

www.peacealchemist.com

The contents of this book should not be considered a prescription or medical advice for any disease. I suggest you consult a naturopath from a multi-year doctorate college program* or a physician with a background in natural medicine before proceeding with any regimen that affects your health.**

There are innumerable naturopath internet programs. Use ample discernment when taking advice from someone with this as their training.

**A word of caution when using the internet to research nutrition, detoxing, or anything else: While writing this book, I found several articles that claimed there was research to support a claim. There were no references, and when I tried to find support for their claim, there was none I could locate.*

Dedication: I dedicate this book to the dear beings watching and supporting my work on the other side of the veil. I often feel and hear you nearby.

Acknowledgments

Invaluable feedback, validation, and suggestions from the people listed below helped shape this book into a powerful guide for your Inner Peace Journey.

Jim Adcock

Andy Dutschman

Sue Healy

Pat & Kitty Shirk

Shelley Lynn Hines

Nikki Moore

Nathan Townley

Christina Averhart

Opening the third eye is a sacred process. You will receive wisdom beyond the mundane when the third eye is open. You must travel the sacred journey to inner peace to 'know' without filters, to 'know' with understanding, to 'know' with compassion, to 'know' peace, and to 'know' the unity of the one heart.

Contents

Introduction 1
Part I: Tools and Guides for Healing Your Intuition 9
   Chapter 1: How to Use This Book 11
   Chapter 2: Grounding 16
   Chapter 3: The Wording and Source of Emotional States 18
      The Wording of Emotional Patterns 18
      The Source of Emotional Patterns 20
   Chapter 4: The Work 21
   Chapter 5: Remen Q̄ 23
      Remen Q̄ Introduction 23
      The Remen Q̄ Process 25
      IONS (A Shortcut) 26
      Website Link 27
      Subtle Energy Body and Remen Q̄ 28
      The Remen Q̄ Contradiction 29
   Chapter 6: Remen Q̄ Session Script Examples 30
      The Remen Q̄ Session with Leaning-In and the Source is Unknown 31
      The Remen Q̄ Session Without Leaning-In 33
      The Remen Q̄ Session with Leaning-In and the Source is Known 34
      The Remen Q̄ Session with Ancestral Method, Leaning-In and the Source is Unknown 36
Part II: Metaphysical Exploration of the Third Eye Chakra 40
   Chapter 7: The Third Eye 41
   Chapter 8: Developing Your Intuition 46
      Awareness Exercises 48
      Develop Calmness 50

- Boundaries 51
- Intuitive Question Process 52
- Discernment 53
- Helpful Hints 58

Chapter 9: The Stages of Intuition Development 61
- Survival Stage 63
- Creation Stage 75
- Dancing with the Ego 82
- Self-Realization 88

Chapter 10: The Clairs 90
- Clair Wounding 92

Chapter 11: The Wounded Intuitive 95
- Symptoms of a Wounded Intuitive 97
- Emotional Patterns: The Wounded Intuitive 98
- Blocks to Intuition 103

Chapter 12: Pineal Gland Wellness and Third Eye Activation 110
- Supporting Pineal Gland Wellness 111
- How Do You Know if Your Third Eye is Opening and Activated? 113

Glossary 115

Resources 124
- Body Scans 124
- Emotional Patterns 125
- Grounding Meditation 126
- Journaling 127
- Leaning-In 130

About the Author 132

Contacting Valeria and Additional Support 134

Appendices 135
- Appendix A: About the Pineal Gland 136
  - What and Where is the Pineal Gland? 136

What Does the Pineal Gland Do? 137

Working with Emotional Patterns and Emotional Pathophysiology ... 139

Appendix B: Physical Diseases, Disorders and the Associated Emotional Patterns of the Pineal Gland 140

Advanced Sleep Phase Disorder (ASPD) 141

Delayed Sleep Phase Disorder (DSPD) 144

Fluoride Toxicity 147

Hypermelatoninemia 151

Hypomelatoninemia 154

Pineal Gland Calcification 157

Pineal Gland Cysts 160

Pineal Gland Tumor 163

Pineocytoma 166

Seasonal Affective Disorder 169

Appendix C: Physical Diseases and Disorders Associated with an Impaired Pineal Gland and the Emotional Patterns 172

Alzheimer's Disease 173

Anxiety 178

Depression 182

Depression with a History of Abuse 188

Huntington's Disease 191

Insomnia 195

Insulin Resistance 198

Lupus 201

Migraines 206

Motor neuron disease (ALS) 209

Multiple Sclerosis 212

Parkinson's Disease 215

Schizophrenia 219

Stroke 221

Sexual dysfunction (as it pertains to the pineal gland) 223

Appendix D: Physiology and Emotional Pathophysiology of the Pineal Gland 226

    Function: Regulates the Circadian Rhythm and Sleep Cycles 227

    Emotional Pathophysiology: Dysregulated Circadian Rhythm and Sleep Cycles Related to Low Melatonin...227

    Function: Strengthens the Immune System 231

    Emotional Pathophysiology: A Weakened Immune System Related to Low Melatonin 231

    Function: Crucial for Reducing the Risk of Cancer...........................234

    Emotional Pathophysiology: Elevated Risk of Cancer Because of Low Melatonin 234

    Function: Melatonin Increases Bone Regeneration.........................237

    Emotional Pathophysiology: Decreased Bone Regeneration Because of Low Melatonin...237

    Function: Protecting Against Oxidative Stress 240

    Emotional Pathophysiology: Impaired Protection Against Oxidative Stress Because of Low Melatonin..240

    Function: Improves Neurogenesis and Synaptic Plasticity 243

    Emotional Pathophysiology: Impaired Neurogenesis and Synaptic Plasticity Because of Low Melatonin. 243

    Function: Suppressing Neuroinflammation 246

    Emotional Pathophysiology: Impaired Neuroinflammation Suppression Because of Low Melatonin...247

    Function: Modulates the Immune Response 249

    Emotional Pathophysiology: Unmodulated Immune Response Because of Low Melatonin...249

    Function: Enhancing Memory Function..252

    Emotional Pathophysiology: Impaired Memory Function Because of Low Melatonin 252

    Function: Plays a Role in Spatial Navigation....................................255

    Emotional Pathophysiology: Impaired Spatial Navigation 255

    Function: Controlling the Timing and Release of Female and Male Reproductive Hormones 257

Emotional Pathophysiology: Dysregulated Timing and Release of Female and Male Reproductive Hormones 257

Function: Restores the body 260

Emotional Pathophysiology: Lack of Body Restoration Because of Low Melatonin 260

Function: Regulation of the Pituitary Gland 263

Emotional Pathophysiology: Dysregulated Pituitary Gland Because of Low Melatonin 263

Function: Glucose Homeostasis and Energy Balance 267

Emotional Pathophysiology: Unbalanced Glucose Homeostasis and Energy Due to Low Melatonin 267

Function: DNA Repair 270

Emotional Pathophysiology: Impaired DNA Repair Due to Low Melatonin 270

Introduction

Imagine a life where choices flow effortlessly, anxieties melt away, and you navigate the world with a quiet inner knowing. This way of being isn't magic; it's the power of a healed intuition. This workbook's tools, processes, and information make a healed intuition possible.

This book is for the spiritual seeker and journeyer striving to achieve Inner Peace. It underscores the pivotal role of intuition and offers profound insights for your Inner Peace Journey*. This book is designed to assist anyone in pursuit of consistent and harmonious intuitive guidance toward inner peace; it emphasizes the importance of maintaining a healthy pineal gland and transcending limiting patterns that obstruct the flow of information.

See Glossary page 120. A brief glossary of fundamental terms is provided for additional support starting on page 115.

The Inner Peace Journey takes you to who you are.

Some of you come to this book feeling lost and stuck. Possibly, your creativity is frozen; a book is not getting written, or an engineering project is not moving forward. You may have an overall feeling of not leading an authentic life. The thing to remember is that you start where you are right now. This book will assist you wherever you are in the Inner Peace Journey. This book is best used as a workbook to facilitate the transmutation* of intuition blocks to a flow of intuitive information as you move along this path.

See Glossary page 122 for more information.

Have you experienced:

- Trouble sleeping?
- Vision problems or sinus problems?
- Feeling overwhelmed when you go into a store with many people?

- Feeling life has no magic or joy?
- Migraines?
- Feeling your life has yet to realize a purpose?
- Feeling lost? Feeling stuck?
- Sensing the feelings of others and making them your own?
- Are you seen as having shortcomings?
- Quickly dropping into thinking the worst outcomes will happen?
- Being often misled by perceptions?
- Distrusting your inner voice?
- Getting stuck in the creative process?
- Facing repeated undesired situations?
- Facing repeated undesired relationships?
- Unable to turn off the inner chatter?
- Spending hundreds and maybe thousands of dollars on "manifesting" classes, and the only thing you manifested was a reduced bank account and frustration?

Do You have:

- Difficulty making timely business decisions?
- Rigid, parental or ancestral thinking?
- Difficulty solving problems?
- Impaired creativity?
- A tendency to shift easily into states of non-peace?
- Resistance to completing personal projects?
- Trouble making business decisions?
- Difficulty giving or receiving?

Your intuition is impaired if you answered yes to one or more of the questions above. Your third eye chakra* may be out of balance, and the pineal gland may be physically impaired. The Pineal gland is a connection between the physical and spiritual world. Many spiritual traditions refer to the pineal gland as the seat of the soul. Metaphysically and physiologically, the pineal gland, as an endocrine gland, is about control and regulation. Control and regulation at the emotional level is about being in control or out of control of the various aspects of your life to be safe. For example, you may work for a boss that micro-manages everything they are responsible for. For your boss, this behavior is essential to feel safe. Do you need to have a project's details nailed down to feel safe?

See Glossary page 116 for more information.

The pineal gland, known as the third eye due to containing light-sensitive photoreceptors[1], was aligned with the third eye chakra when the Western concept of chakras was developed in the 1920s. **A seven-chakra system was developed that aligned the seven major chakras with an endocrine gland**. This body of esoteric thought was an unintentional collaborative development by The Theosophical Society, Carl Jung, Charles W. Leadbetter, Joseph Campbell, Indian Tantrism and more[2].

Physiologically, the pineal gland, as an endocrine gland, controls and regulates many body functions. For example, melatonin is a hormone produced by the pineal gland. Melatonin controls sleep, bone regeneration, the immune response and more. The following limiting patterns (fears, beliefs/created patterns, and emotional states) may be the result of a pineal gland imbalance:

- Too much or too little control
- Dysregulation of emotions
- Impatience, lack of discernment
- Feelings of worthlessness
- An imbalance in giving and receiving
- Feelings of being not good enough or unacceptable

The balance of giving and receiving reflects the flow of life force. Resistance to the flow of life force will affect the flow of money, the ability to manifest, physical and emotional renewal, experiencing joy, and more. The vibrational frequency of these limiting emotional patterns may create a con-

---

[1] Vigh, B., Manzano, M. J., Zádori, A., Frank, C. L., Lukáts, A., Röhlich, P., Szél, A., & Dávid, C. (2002). Nonvisual Photoreceptors of the Deep Brain, Pineal Organs and Retina. *Histology and Histopathology*, 17(2), 555–590. Available from https://doi.org/10.14670/HH-17.555

[2] Contributors to Wikimedia projects. (2024, April 4). *Chakra*. Wikipedia. Available from https://en.wikipedia.org/wiki/Chakra

traction that blocks the flow of life force and impairs the third eye chakra and the pineal gland.

The catalyst for writing this book was a request from an acquaintance to open his third eye. I did an energetic opening of his chakras. After I left my acquaintance, I heard my inner voice tell me that this was only temporary and that the effect would fade. I then "knew" that this would require more than a temporary chakra adjustment. It would also require the following:

- The transmutation of limiting emotional patterns
- Detoxification of the pineal gland
- Reduction of exposure to fluoride in food, water, medicine, and cooking utensils
- A spiritual practice

I also knew this needed to be one of the first things people must do on their journey toward inner peace. **The Inner Peace Journey requires knowing and insight**. The insights of a higher knowing will facilitate the development of understanding, more profound compassion and a heart at peace.

Writing this book became a proving ground for this work. I would transmute the limiting patterns in Part Two and the Appendices that triggered me as I wrote. I encountered situations that highlighted my intuitive wounds and the constriction caused by recognizing limiting patterns. One such experience occurred during a trip to California with my partner. As I drove, I asked myself, "How will I know if the pineal gland detoxing efforts and the transmutation of limiting patterns were working? I felt intuitive already; how would I know there was a difference?" When we reached Medford, Oregon, we checked into a hotel. My sweetie's level of resilience after a few hours of travel was gone. When I entered the room, an area by the front door smelled like rotting flesh. The flooring was damaged in that spot, and it indicated to me that blood had seeped into the subflooring below. The smell was very pronounced. But the smell did not extend beyond that space. At that moment, I needed to consider my options. I knew Mike would not move rooms. His sense of smell was gone, and he had no energy to consider moving rooms. So, I convinced Mike that we should get dinner; this would give me time to think. After ordering our meal, I told Mike I needed to return to the room for medicine.

I was getting space to reflect on the situation. I began by using Remen Q̄[3] (see page 25 for instructions) to transmute the relationship that brought that experience—then I surrounded the area in layers of different light colors, with the last layer being heart energy. My inner guidance told me this would only hold until morning. The smell was gone after Remen Q̄'ing the relationship and light layering the area. As I was checking out the following day, I told the desk clerk there was a smell of rot in the room. She immediately got defensive and said no one died in that room. I then said something I had never said to anyone. I told her I was intuitive and could sense energies others may not. I was surprised at myself for saying that. She laughed at me and rolled her eyes. Later, as I reflected on the event. I could not understand why I had said what I said. I would never have declared my intuitive abilities in that way. I asked myself why I had responded reactively to her disbelief. I felt the humiliation, ridicule and rejection in my heart, but there was another level of awareness.

This new awareness was how I kept myself small. I was afraid of being who I "am." I was afraid of the ridicule and diminishment of others. So, I worked to keep myself hidden. Keeping myself small does not help me or those who resonate with my work. I was afraid of being rejected, ridiculed, wrong and humiliated, which resulted in keeping myself in the shadows. I was holding this in my pineal gland. This event was the answer to my question. Keeping myself small and in **control** of my smallness was the resulting emotional state from these fears.

A few months after the Medford incident, another profound example of the changes I had made while writing the material in this book entered my awareness. I taught Reiki I to one student. After completing the attunement, the student used me as her first Reiki practice. I experienced the flow of the universal life force as I had never experienced it before. I felt a strong, energetic flow through the nadis (see Glossary page 121) and chakras (see Glossary page 116) in my entire body. At the end of the session, I felt joyous and ecstatic. The joy continued for several days, and a feeling of compassion and patience permeated daily life. I have been receiving and giving Reiki and many other energy modalities since the early 2000s,

---

[3] Moore, Valeria (2021). *The Remen Q̄ Method: An Easy Do It Yourself Process to Create Inner Peace and Change Your Reality*. Keizer, Oregon, USA; Three Moons Publishing

and I have never experienced anything like this. The transmutation work with Remen Q̄ I had been doing while writing this book had worked to remove energetic contraction and devitalization throughout my body. For me, this is a new way of being in the world. This persistent state of joy is our natural state.

Over the months, I have experienced a heightened awareness and life force. My intuition felt more grounded. There was a flow and ease to my work. I became more peaceful and patient amid many daily challenges. I began to become more fully engaged with my intuitive skills. In the past, I have rarely used my intuition for myself. I started asking questions that would have intuitive answers about me. Asking these questions helped me disconnect from an exploitative relationship and develop the next level of compassion.

In Part I, you will learn about suggestions for detoxing your pineal gland, exercises for activating your third eye, tools for transmuting your limiting emotional patterns and how to use those tools. You will learn why you should work with an emotional release therapy* that does **not** replace one pattern for another, for example, Remen Q̄. Included are the instructions for Remen Q̄ and sample session scripts to facilitate your transmutation work.

*See Glossary page 117 for more information.

Part II explores third-eye metaphysics, stages of intuition development, the limiting patterns of the wounded empath, the wounded intuitive and blocks to intuition. Most people poorly understand intuition and regard it with suspicion, anger and hate. For centuries, institutions have worked to shut down anyone who presents intuitive thoughts or actions. As a consequence, we experience emotional wounding that blocks our intuition. If you grew up in a dysfunctional home, you might have used your intuitive abilities for survival. If so, you probably became a wounded empath.

Additionally, Part II delves into the fears, emotional states, and limiting created patterns you may hold related to intuition or the pineal gland. Reading the material in those chapters is designed to create an awareness of what you may be holding that blocks your intuition. You are being triggered (see Glossary page 122 for more information) when you have a physical or emotional response after reading one of the statements. This contraction is your cue to transmute the non-peace that has been triggered to peace. A contraction may appear as a slight ache, a sharp pain, or an unease.

Appendices A, B, C and D are optional resources for your Inner Peace Journey. Appendix A explains the physiology of the pineal gland. Appendixes B and C examine the limiting emotional patterns for diseases relating directly and indirectly to the pineal gland. A disease can be multifaceted in its connections within the body, i.e., it involves many other organs and functions. For example, Parkinson's disease is complex, and there is a component that may link to the pineal gland, but there are also other structures in the brain, gut, etc., that may be complicit in the development of the disease.[4,5]

A new level of limiting patterns, called emotional pathophysiology, is presented for the first time in Appendix D. Emotional pathophysiology is a deeper, more fundamental level of limiting patterns potentially leading to pineal gland pre-disease dysfunction. A function is specific to one aspect of the pineal gland, such as generating melatonin to suppress inflammation.[6] The emotional pathophysiology then shows up as dysfunctional immune suppression involving the pineal gland.

The journey to inner peace may be a path of small incremental changes for some people; for others, it may be giant leaps. I am not promising you will wake up an intuitive or spiritually enlightened being tomorrow. I am offering tools, processes and information for your Inner Peace Journey. How you make the journey is up to you. But as you transmute limiting patterns, your life will go from being contracted around your wounds, story and identity to one that is expansive and embodies a consistent inner peace. Your life will change. These changes will bring lightness and joy into your life. You will expand into the light you are. You may see yourself become

---

[4] Gallop A, Weagley J, Paracha S-R, Grossberg G. The Role of The Gut Microbiome in Parkinson's Disease. *Journal of Geriatric Psychiatry and Neurology.* 2021;34(4):253-262. Available from doi:10.1177/08919887211018268

[5] Payami H, Zareparsi S. Genetic Epidemiology of Parkinson's Disease. *Journal of Geriatric Psychiatry and Neurology.* 1998;11(2):98-106. Available from doi:10.1177/089198879801100207

[6] Won, E., Na, K. S., & Kim, Y. K. (2021). Associations between Melatonin, Neuroinflammation, and Brain Alterations in Depression. *International Journal of Molecular Sciences*, 23(1), 305. Available from https://doi.org/10.3390/ijms23010305

more authentic, you may have access to previously unavailable information, you may respond non-reactively, you may be aware of choices that give you peace and add more meaning to your life.

> *What we call "the divine," is none other than the energy of awakening, of peace, of understanding, and of love, which is to be found not only in every human being but in every species on Earth. ~Thich Nhat Hanh*

You picked up this book because you got my email, read a website, a friend suggested it, or saw a social media post and felt the pull to know more. You may have read through the symptoms of an impaired third eye chakra or pineal gland and resonated with the statements. **When you feel that compelling call to know more, you are getting a message from your higher self that you need to ask more questions and follow where the answers lead you.** The information in this book helps you recognize the wounds you carry that stop you from gaining the insight you need along your journey to peace.

Part I: Tools and Guides for Healing Your Intuition

Are you ready for the next step in your spiritual journey?

Chapter 1: How to Use This Book

You may have scanned through this book and are ready to jump in and do the transmutation work. Before starting the actual journey of transmutation with the material in this book, please do the following:

Use a transmutational/emotional release process to transmute your wounding to neutral or peace. I suggest Remen Q̄. You may have a process that you are familiar with. Please be sure you are not setting up a bypass*. Replacing a limiting pattern with another (modality** of duality) will create a bypass and a limiting pattern, maybe many limiting patterns.

See Glossary page 115 for more information.

**See Glossary page 121 for more information.*

Remen Q̄ is about peace. When doing Remen Q̄, you transmute, with intention, for peace and only peace. With Remen Q̄, the intention for peace will create balance in your energy fields.* If you set an intention for anything other than peace, then you are creating a non-resolving non-peace that is not Remen Q̄.

See Chapter 5 page 28 for more information.

Remen Q̄[7] transmutes a relationship to peace. The state of peace allows the contracted limiting pattern and non-peace relationship to flow life force where it had once been impaired or slowed.

Remen Q̄ has several advantages:

- No digging (which can be endless). Digging is a term used to describe making assumptions or asking questions to find the origin of a trauma.
- No muscle testing (which can be inaccurate – see page 76).*
- Does not create additional bypasses (which can create un-wellness)
- Has a process for transmuting existing bypasses

---

[7] Moore, V. (2021). *The Remen Q̄ Method: An Easy Do-It-Yourself Process to Create Inner Peace and Change Your Reality.* Three Moons Publishing.

- Transmutes – which raises you to a higher state of peace and balance
- You don't need to know the origin
- You don't need to tell a story (this just reinforces the trauma)
- It makes a big difference in how happy and fulfilled you feel.
- A state of peace harmonizes energy systems
- The intention is ALWAYS peace
- Heart-based – which is the portal to your soul's wisdom
- It is based on an ancient wisdom of ascension

It is outside the scope of this book to delve into muscle testing.

The Remen $\overline{Q}$[8] book covers the Remen $\overline{Q}$ Method in more detail and can be purchased from your local bookstore or Amazon.

If you have another modality* you are working with, check to see if it is non-dualistic. Duality, as it applies to emotional release work, would be a process of replacing one thing for another. For example, you replace "I'm not good enough" with "I'm good enough." This replacement creates a duality and a bypass. Replacement will create imbalances in the physical, emotional, subtle** and mental bodies. Some healing modalities work temporarily. For example, some energetic techniques will temporarily relieve the emotional or physical pain you are experiencing. Then, in some period, the issue is back; this is a bypass.

*See Glossary page 121 for more information.

**Nadis (channels for life force or meridians) and chakras are aspects of the subtle energy body. A detailed discussion of the subtle energy body is outside the purview of this book. See page 28 in Chapter 5 for more information.

Have a journal to write your discoveries and progress. Journaling is a way to achieve self-awareness. Self-awareness allows you to understand your nature by being the witness to your life. The process of self-awareness asks that we not judge ourselves or engage in self-criticism.

Check-in daily with your journal to create a space for all the thoughts running around in your head. It's OK that they may not make any sense. If the thoughts are limiting, use Remen $\overline{Q}$ to transmute them to peace. Af-

---

[8] Moore, Valeria (2021). *The Remen $\overline{Q}$ Method: An Easy Do It Yourself Process to Create Inner Peace and Change Your Reality.* Keizer, Oregon, USA; Three Moons Publishing

ter the initial daily check-in with your thoughts, check-in with your heart. Is there something bothering you? Is your heart contracted? This state of awareness is what I call journal meditation. After writing my question, I hold my pencil to the paper, close my eyes for a moment and allow information to flow. This process may take some practice. I will hear a couple of words that may make no sense initially. Write down the impressions or what you hear. Don't judge; allow, observe, write and transmute.

When you journal, you listen to your heart's transmission of wisdom beyond your logical thinking processes. When you access wisdom beyond the boundaries of the logical mind, you will discover knowledge beyond the logical mind. This type of information is beyond fear. You can ask for guidance from this aspect of self that you encounter beyond these boundaries. When you do this, write the question and then write down what comes to mind. Doing so will give you an anchor for reflection and possible emotional release work.

Journaling allows you to focus your thoughts and yields insights into the limiting patterns you may be holding. Your awareness of what you hold develops as you write those limiting patterns. Once you are aware of limiting patterns, you have a choice. You may choose to transmute those limiting patterns or not. Choosing not to transmute limiting patterns means you will experience those patterns again.

Make sure you date the entries. Journaling will allow you to track your progress and revisit remaining contractions caused by a limiting pattern.

Journaling allows you to transmute as you write; this is a gift of the journaling process. As you write, you are listening with your heart and that listening can create the transmutation of pain.

Some people have difficulty journaling. I have been recommending Julia Cameron's <u>The Artist's Way: A Spiritual Path to Higher Creativity</u>[9] since it was first published in 1992. In Ms. Cameron's book, she presents methods and practices for breaking through the blocks of journaling. I suggest coupling practices presented in <u>The Artist's Way</u> with Remen $\bar{Q}$ to transmute the emotional blocks that are triggered.

---

[9] Cameron, J. (2020). *The Artist's Way: A Spiritual Path to Higher Creativity*. Souvenir Press.

Do not use a text-to-speech reader. The created patterns, fears, and emotional states are meant to be read individually and reflected upon. There is a vibrational frequency with the limiting patterns that needs to come through your inner voice, not the one provided by a software programmer. If you must use a reader, repeat the limiting patterns in your inner voice and feel the body experience after repeating the limiting pattern.

The suggested approach below combines skill building and transmuting the emotional wounds you may be holding that block your intuition. The Inner Peace Journey is very personal and non-linear.

Material from the Emotional Patterns and The Remen Q̄ Method books is included throughout this book, so you do not have to purchase additional resources to do the exercises in this book.

Suggested Approach

1. Read the introduction.

2. Become familiar with the inner wisdom tools of grounding, journaling and meditation. Practice journaling and meditation daily.

3. Learn Remen Q̄.

4. Read Part I before proceeding to Part II.

5. Remove as much fluoride as possible from your life (see Supporting Pineal Gland Wellness on page 111) and use detoxing methods.

6. After reading through Part II, begin doing the Awareness Exercises in Chapter 8.

7. Start working with the Intuitive Question Process on page 52. Journal the information you receive. Evaluate the information you receive: What is the feeling? Can the information be verified? Is it compassionate? Is the information helpful? You may want to do this daily. You are building a skill. Skills take practice.

8. Go back periodically and redo the pineal gland scan*. Note in your journal the changes you experience in your pineal gland.

    The pineal gland scan is explored in Awareness Exercise #2 on page 48 in Chapter 8.

9. In your daily journaling, ask, "What do I notice that is different about myself?" Journal your response. Ask this question once a month or more often until you feel you have a sense of your intuition and how it works for you. You may not get an answer right away. The answer to this question may unfold.

10. Depending on the changes you perceive, you may want to go back and review the fears, created patterns and emotional states in Chapters 9 through 11. Check for bypasses by leaning-in. The Glossary explains bypasses. The Resources chapter explains leaning-in.

11. Read through the Appendices and transmute any patterns that create a contraction.

12. Learn Reiki and get a Reiki 1 attunement. Learning to meditate started my Inner Peace Journey, and Reiki gave me new energy and direction for my path. The Reiki attunement facilitated the activation of my third eye. The healing of my wounded intuition would unfold over the years.

Chapter 2: Grounding

While doing the transmutation work, you will need to be grounded. Being ungrounded will sabotage your efforts. If you become ungrounded while engaging in this material, step back from the transmutation work and reground yourself. You may even need a sleep cycle away from the journey work. A sleep cycle will rebalance your body and mind. While writing this book, I often encountered limiting patterns I needed to transmute. My ungrounded response was sleepiness. Often, that feeling was so profound all I could do was honor the feeling and take a nap. I would then Remen $\bar{Q}$ the feeling of sleepiness. Use sleepiness as a point of non-peace and use Remen $\bar{Q}$ to transmute.

Symptoms of being ungrounded:

- ✦ Unfocused
- ✦ Unable to remember the details
- ✦ Clumsy: You drop things or run into the corners of furniture and walls
- ✦ Trying to do too much at once
- ✦ Looping negative thoughts
- ✦ Sleepy or fatigued
- ✦ Someone talks to you, and you immediately feel overwhelmed and become reactive.
- ✦ You are detached and numb.
- ✦ Anxious
- ✦ Feeling disconnected from yourself, others, and the world around you
- ✦ A floaty feeling; feet feel like you aren't connecting to the earth

Suggestions for grounding:

1. Start by using Remen $\bar{Q}$ to transmute the feeling of being ungrounded. Being ungrounded is a state of non-peace.
2. If you are having looping thoughts, do Remen $\bar{Q}$ until you reach a place of peace.
3. Give yourself some time in nature. Take your shoes off and place your feet on the ground if possible. While doing that, imagine breathing in and out of your feet. Imagine the air coming up through your

body as you inhale and then down your body as you exhale. Be present to the feelings in your feet. Feel the wet sand, grass, water, rocks or dirt under your feet. Tell yourself how that feels. Hug a tree. Listen to the tree.
4. Practice a grounding meditation (see page 126).
5. Dance. The movement brings you into feeling your body. Use whatever music brings you a connection with your body. The movement will also move excess energy that may make you anxious or stressed.
6. Eat root vegetables: carrots, beets, parsnips, radishes, sweet potatoes, potatoes, etc.
7. Take a nap. The nap need only be 15-20 minutes. Then you can Remen $\bar{Q}$, the limiting pattern(s) that triggered the feeling of being ungrounded.

Chapter 3: The Wording and Source of Emotional States

The Wording of Emotional Patterns

One of my favorite mind-body authors, Annette Noontil, wrote in a way that requires the reader to sit with the information and see what it means at a deeper level. She wrote; <u>The Body is the Barometer of the Soul, So Be Your Own Doctor.</u>[10] She would offer one word or a phrase, and the reader would need to sit with the information and determine what that meant to them. The wording of this book's emotional states in Part II and the Appendices may require the reader to 'sit' with the writing. If the wording feels cryptic, close your eyes, holding the relevant phrase in your mind, and ask, 'What does this mean to me?' or 'What would be another way of stating this?' The answer will be what is correct for you. In some cases, I have added a note to give an example of how an emotional state may have appeared in a person's life.

Grammatically, the emotional patterns material is not proper English. The sentences are sometimes incomplete. The language used may seem improper. Punctuation can seem wrong. These grammar errors are **not** incorrect. There is a resonance, a vibration, to the wording. The wording may resonate with a wound you hold. The wording may slow you down so that you have time to feel what is being presented. After you read a limiting pattern and feel a contraction, your body signals that you are holding a limiting pattern. **You do not need to know what the source of the contraction is or where it came from.** You can use the experience of the contraction as the point of non-peace and transmute it with Remen $\bar{Q}$. With Remen $\bar{Q}$, the contraction you feel is the measurement of peace or non-peace.

---

[10] Noontil, Annette(2000). *The Body is the Barometer of the Soul: So be Your Own Doctor.* Nunawading, Vic.; Australia; Self-Published.

The emotional patterns are not definitive. There are possibly many more emotional states, fears, or created patterns that align with a specific disease or physiological function that are not listed.

The Source of Emotional Patterns

The most common question about emotional patterns writing is, "What is the source of emotional patterns?" The source is Universal Wisdom. Universal Wisdom is also known as the Time Continuum, Akashic Record and the Zero Point. Universal Wisdom is akin to a library of vibrational frequencies that are recordings of all that has happened and possibilities in the universe. To access this information, I go into a light meditation and use an intuitive process to ask my questions. There are no other beings or personalities involved.

Chapter 4: The Work

Transmutation work is a journey. Progress toward inner peace happens by doing the Inner Peace Journey Work.* Sometimes, the work is hard. You can proactively address limiting patterns or let the Universe hit you with the cosmic two-by-four**. When the Universe brings your attention to a limiting pattern, you can ignore it, but the cosmic two-by-four will happen again until you transmute the limiting pattern. I speak from experience.

See Glossary page120 for more information.

**The cosmic two-by-four phrase describes an event that draws your attention to something that needs to happen for continued growth on your life path. For example, you get laid off from a toxic job, the cosmic two-by-four, and your inner voice has prompted you to quit long before being laid off, but you ignored the advice.*

When working with the limiting patterns in this book, give yourself a moment to check in with your body. Is there a contraction in your heart? Is there a new tightness in your body? Is there a new discomfort or pain in your body? If there is, then stop, note it in your journal and Remen Q̄ the fear, created pattern or emotional state until you reach a place of peace. Then, record the result in your journal*

See page 127 for more information.

Journaling allows you to focus your thoughts and yields insights into the limiting patterns you may be holding. When journaling, you may record your feelings and behaviors that limit you. Your awareness of what you hold develops as you write those limiting patterns. Once you are aware of limiting patterns, you have a choice. You may choose to transmute those limiting patterns or not.

After your initial journal entry, lean-into* the limiting pattern and check if more Remen Q̄ work is needed. For example, as I worked on a section of this book, I felt an intense achy pinch at the base of my neck and the top of my shoulder. The ache went up the side of my neck into the base of my skull. One of the limiting patterns triggered a recognition that I felt unsupported in carrying a heavy load, and there was no one to ask for help. This feeling was a childhood wounding of knowing and clairempathy.

I Remen Q̄ 'd the created pattern, and the dull ache dissolved, and I felt at peace.[11]

See page 130 for more information.

A numb heart or body is a state of non-peace. Some of the limiting patterns in this book you may have experienced many times, yet when you read the limiting pattern statement, you don't feel a contraction. Over time, the contraction may become a disease or disorder, and you have numbed out the emotional response. Using Remen Q̄, transmute the limiting pattern of numbness to peace.*

See Chapter 5 for more information.

It's been my experience that much of the wounding held by the pineal gland and the third eye is familial, epigenetic or ancestral. **This means the limiting pattern may have shown up in your life in varying vibrational frequencies with the same label. Still, each experience of the limiting pattern has a different vibrational frequency**. For example, you have had a recent experience of being betrayed at work by a coworker. As a child, you felt betrayed by a parent. The relationship with a parent is very different from that with a coworker. Hence, the vibrational frequency of the wound will be different. The pattern of betrayal may have originated with an ancestor, and you inherited an ancestral pattern of betrayal. Each of these experiences holds the wound of betrayal at its core, yet each has a different vibrational frequency. You will need to transmute these emotional wounds separately or use the leaning-in process*.

See page 130 for more information.

---

[11] Moore, V. (2020). Intuition Wounding. Available from https://emotionalpatterns.com/intuition-wounding/

Chapter 5: Remen Q̄

Remen Q̄ Introduction

Remen Q̄ is a simple four-step process to achieve inner peace. Below is a portion of the introduction from the Remen Q̄ book and the process.

*"**The Remen Q̄ Method will bring peace to your heart if you own your non-peace, and peace is your intention.** You take ownership of the non-peace when you acknowledge that you are the creator of your non-peace. Owning your non-peace does not mean you are responsible for the wounding. It means there is a relationship, a connection to the source of the non-peace. There is no fault or blame in this process. You are taking ownership of the relationship. Once you have taken ownership, you have already begun transmuting the non-peace.*

***When you live with peace in your heart, you open yourself to being present; you open yourself to living in the moment.** By being present in the moment, you no longer live a reactive, fear-based existence. By living from presence, you change your reality. When you experience heart peace, you extend that feeling to those who may have been the mirror to your fear. You then empower others to move beyond the limitations of fear-based identities. When you live from a place of peace in your heart, creativity and inspiration flow into your life. Your peace becomes my peace.*

***The Remen Q̄ Method offers you 'a way' of living that brings you peace and presence.** Your presence in the world will change as you go from reactive to being present and non-reactive. The more present you are, the more you become aware of the limiting patterns you created. Once those limiting patterns and associated relationships change to peace, you free up energy for living. The energy trapped in limiting patterns is now free to create and experience joy. Creative and joyful energy becomes the physical change that supports a life of flow.*

***Your heart is much more than just a muscle.** Your heart is an energetic center with a bridge or portal to the soul's universal wisdom, the Akasha.*

Your heart is the first organ in your body to develop. Your heart, in a state of peace, has an intuitive sense of knowing. Your heart is a center of consciousness that sends and receives information to the thinking-mind and body-mind. Your heart is the sender and receiver of information to other sentient beings. Your heart differentiates between peace and non-peace feelings. Your heart is the seat of the experience of 'Kibriya,' divine joy. Kibriya (pronounced kih-bree-yuh) is a knowing of oneness and a feeling of love of all.

*I learned of Kibriya from Andrew Harvey during a course on Rumi at Wisdom University, now Ubiquity University.

Remen Q̄ is not about controlling the future. *It is not about manifesting wealth. It is not about controlling others. It is not about forcing a specific outcome. It is not about changing one belief for another. It is not about instantaneous healing of a physical disorder.* **Remen Q̄ is about inner peace.**

If you want a life of inner peace, Remen Q̄ brings you inner peace when non-peace is triggered. **Achieving a life of continuous, uninterrupted peace requires that you commit to the inner work.** *First, you must own your reality. You must own that you created your reality. Then, use the tools that will bring into your awareness the layers of non-peace created by separation systems: family, institutions, government, corporations, religion, education, etc. Once you know the filters these systems of control have instilled within you, your inner work will move you beyond the filters placed on your perceptions by those systems."* [12]

---

[12] Moore, Valeria (2021). *The Remen Q̄ Method: An Easy Do It Yourself Process to Create Inner Peace and Change Your Reality.* Keizer, Oregon, USA; Three Moons Publishing

The Remen Q̄ Process[13]

Close your eyes and place your fingertips on your heart space. Then, <u>breathe into presence</u> by taking five slow, deep breaths through your nose and out through your nose without pausing using tummy breathing.

1. *I am witness to the field of intention to neutralize this created pattern. (Say this in your inner voice.)*

2. *I am witness to the origins of this created pattern*

   (Say this in your inner voice and visualize a representation of the origin. Do not overthink the image. Make up something. That something will carry the vibrational frequency of the non-peace.)

3. *I am witness to the neutralization of this created pattern. (Say this in your inner voice and visualize a change in the image. Halfway through visualizing the change, **snap** open your eyes.)*

4. *Now close your eyes and move your attention to your body and watch until you feel it is complete. (If there is a sensation of lightheadedness or swirling, allow the sensation to finish.)*

---

[13] Moore, Valeria (2021). *The Remen Q̄ Method: An Easy Do It Yourself Process to Create Inner Peace and Change Your Reality.* Keizer, Oregon, USA; Three Moons Publishing

IONS (A Shortcut)

If you have difficulty remembering the process, use the acronym IONS.

> I = Intention
>
> O = Origin
>
> N = Neutralization
>
> S = Snap

After breathing into presence with eyes closed, replace the phrases with the word's intention, origin, and neutralization. You may have to do the extended version of the Remen Q̄ process a few times, the non-shortcut method, before using the shortcut.

1. **Intention** *(Say this in your inner voice.)*

2. **Origin** *(Say this in your inner voice and visualize a representation of the origin.)*

3. **Neutralization** *(Say this in your inner voice and visualize a change in the image. Halfway through visualizing the change, <u>**snap**</u> open your eyes.)*

4. *Now close your eyes and move your attention to your body and watch until you feel it is complete. (If there is a sensation of light-headedness or swirling, allow the sensation to finish.)*

Website Link

The following link will take you to a website page guiding you through the Remen Q̄ process.

https://peacealchemist.com/the-remen-q-method/#rqrecording

Subtle Energy Body and Remen Q̄

The subtle energy body is made up of auras, nadis and chakras.* Nadis (also known as meridians) are channels that flow prana, life force energy, within the human body, similar to blood vessels that flow blood. Chakras transmute, distribute and receive prana. When balanced, aligned, and unblocked, energy flows freely through the chakras, harmonizing your body, mind, and spirit. The energy system should be considered as a whole. If one part of the subtle body energy system is out of balance, the whole system is affected. If a nadi or chakra experiences a blockage or impaired flow of prana, physical, mental, and emotional imbalances and disease will result. A chakra will become devitalized when there is a reduced flow of prana. A chakra becomes congested when the outflow of prana from that same chakra is impaired.**

See Glossary page 116 for more information.

**It is outside the scope of this book to explore a comprehensive discussion of the subtle energy body. There are many good resources available on the internet and in book form. I recommend <u>The Chakras and their Functions</u> by Master Choa Kok Sui, <u>The Subtle Body: An Encyclopedia of Your Energetic Anatomy</u> by Cyndi Dale or <u>Hands of Light: A Guide to Healing through the Human Energy Field</u> by Barbara Ann Brennan.

The foundation of Remen Q̄ is peace or non-peace. Non-peace is non-flow and contraction. Remen Q̄ transmutes a state of non-peace to peace(flow). A limiting pattern(s) or instinctual response(s) may result in a contraction. This contraction(s) will be taken on by the subtle, physical, emotional, and mental bodies and develop into imbalances. These imbalances become diseases and disorders.

How does Remen Q̄ affect the subtle energy body? Remen Q̄ transmutes an aspect of the subtle body impairment to flow and peace. Prana will then flow. The swirling or expansive state you may experience with a Remen Q̄ session is the flowing of prana previously blocked by a contracted state of non-peace. The subtle energy body harmonizes and balances its state as part of the transmutation. The unfettered flow of prana is your natural state. In some Remen Q̄ sessions, the sensations will be subtle.

The Remen Q̄ Contradiction

This book lists potential fears, emotional states and created patterns for diseases, pineal gland functions, the wounded empath, spiritual bypass, the wounded intuitive and blocked intuition. But, there's a contradiction; you don't need to know the source of the non-peace with Remen Q̄; you don't need the lists of fears, emotional states and created patterns(beliefs).

So why are those lists there, and why do I keep producing them? The last thing I want people to do is read the lists and Remen Q̄ everything.

Intuitive thinking has been under assault by institutions for thousands of years. These institutions' foundations are built on the need to create humans that conform and comply. As a result, our authentic, intuitive self has been buried by patterns of mistrust, shame, guilt, humiliation, suspicion, not good enough, and more.

The institutions also taught us to 'suck it up,' 'grow up,' 'crying is for babies,' 'keep a stiff upper lip,' etc. The phrases of criticism, sometimes shaming, and judgment were an institutional statement that your hurt feelings were irrelevant and you were to bury the expression of your feelings. As a consequence of burying your feelings, you may have difficulty connecting to the feelings in your heart, which are associated with a limiting pattern.

These lists bring an awareness of what you are holding that blocks your intuition. When read and reflected upon, these lists are meant to trigger a heart or body contraction response of non-peace. Then, once you have an awareness of the limiting pattern, you can choose to transmute to peace.

Chapter 6: Remen Q̄ Session Script Examples

A Remen Q̄ session can be one exercise, and then again, it can be several. It all depends on your heart. Everyone and every session will be different. The following scripts are real examples of the work I have done with Remen Q̄ on myself. The source or story doesn't need to be known, and leaning-in* is not always necessary, although doing that process is never wrong. You only need to know that you are experiencing non-peace, which may be in your body or your heart.

See Resources on page 130.

The example scripts do not include the complete Remen Q̄ process. It is assumed that you have made the witness statements and done the snap.

The Remen Q̄ Session with Leaning-In and the Source is Unknown

In this session, I am using the example of being overwhelmed in Chapter 7 on page 42. Overwhelm is one of the ways I would respond when I was emotionally triggered. Overthinking, overwhelm, procrastination, numbness, people-pleasing, creating chaos, and more are responses to trauma. These responses to trauma will sabotage your Inner Peace Journey Work. I do not know when I started feeling overwhelmed. I remember feeling overwhelmed in my childhood. The feeling of non-peace is present as I begin the Remen Q̄ exercises.

Session

Breathe into presence

1) First Remen Q̄: Origin image of a bright light in a field of dark red.

    Body check-in: There is an 80% reduction in heart contraction.

2) Second Remen Q̄: In the origin image, I felt and saw myself going deep into my heart to a very ancient time. I traveled through a tunnel to a place of sand, giants and primitive humanoids. I was on my stomach with my face in the sand, and the foot of a giant was on my back, grinding my body into the sand.

    Body check-in: There is calm in my heart. But this calm does not feel expansive or light.

3) Third Remen Q̄: In the origin image, I am walking a narrow path through a slot canyon, and I hear, 'yea, though I walk through the valley of the shadow death.'

    Body check-in: There is peace in my heart. But this peace does not feel expansive or light.

4) Fourth Remen $\bar{Q}$: In the origin image, I continue to walk through the slot canyon, and when I reach the other side, I am greeted by a brilliant light.

   Body check-in: My body has a sweet energy of grace and peace.

Result: Since doing this exercise, I have not been overwhelmed.

The Remen Q̄ Session Without Leaning-In

This experience of Remen Q̄ was short, sweet and powerful. I went to the grocery store to pick up a few items for dinner. I selected my food items and went to the checkout line. I was the fourth person in line waiting for checkout. I disappeared into my inner world, disconnected, and did not notice what was transpiring around me. The pain in my knees brought me back to an awareness of the delays at the head of the checkout line. My first awareness was irritation and a growing frustration held by the other people in line. The people holding up the checkout process were being trained by their caretaker to pay for groceries. I could feel the energy of frustration building. People's faces were tight and unhappy. At that moment, I took responsibility for what I sensed in my heart.

I did the following while standing in the grocery line in less than one minute.

Session

Breathe into presence

Remen Q̄ exercise: Origin is the people in line at the grocery store. I felt an unwinding sensation at the snap.

Body check-in: Heart feels peaceful and complete.

Result: My reality shifted. In the next few seconds, the energy shifted around me. People put down their phones and began to talk to one another. I saw smiles and heard laughter. One person recited a funny story. The people in that line started helping each other.

The Remen Q̄ Session with Leaning-In and the Source is Known

I experienced an extraordinary weekend while writing this book. The foundations of my life were gone. My mother died and I discovered my father was probably not my father, and many skeletons had fallen out of the closet. Each skeleton was uglier than the other skeleton. A strange feeling of being unanchored and leaden simultaneously swept over me. As a young girl, I knew of the community whispers, but I did not know the depth of the violence, criminality and hatred that I had lived with.

When I sat to do the Remen Q̄ work on the feeling of non-peace, I heard one word: "silence." I felt the word silence in my heart. Silence felt like shame, so I would not speak. Silence became me disappearing into the background and being quiet. Silence began calling me out to humiliate me.

I had the point of non-peace and the source, which was not necessary to know.* The contracted feeling in my chest and body told me everything I needed to know.

You do not need to know the origin of non-peace. If an image does not appear, make up an image. Do not overthink the origin image. The image could be anything that first comes to mind: a ball, a unicorn, a kitty, etc. The made-up image holds the vibration of the non-peace you are transmuting.

Session

Breathe into presence

1) **First Remen Q̄:** I saw an image of an embryo in the origin step. There is a sense that the trauma was pre-birth and, possibly at conception, ancestral.

    Body check-in: There is a 50% reduction in heart heaviness.

2) Second Remen Q̄: A little girl in a play – being silenced – not being heard as the origin image.

   Body check-in: There is still a slight heaviness in my chest.

3) Third Remen Q̄: A little girl is washing dishes in the origin image. I heard I am the bastard slave.

   Body check-in: There is still a subtle contraction in my chest.

4) Fourth Remen Q̄: An octahedron symbolic shape appeared as the origin. I heard I would always be wrong. I was wrong. I am wrong. I must be silent and unseen. I was the shame.

   Body check-in: At this round, I felt lightness, expansion and joy, yet there was something else. I did not feel the heaviness. I **leaned-into*** my heart, and I felt a knowing that there was still something else. When I **leaned-in,** I moved my focus to my heart region.

See page 130 in Resources for an explanation of how to lean-in.

5) Fifth Remen Q̄: Origin image of being sideswiped.

   Body check-in: I felt another level of expansion, lightness and joy. My chest feels open, peaceful and expansive.

Result: I am still in that space days later.

The Remen Q̄ Session with Ancestral Method, Leaning-In and the Source is Unknown

A dear friend many years ago asked me if my first book, Healer Wisdom* was about me. Without thinking, I answered "yes". While writing this book, I experienced long-buried emotional wounds rising to the surface and getting my attention. One of those long-buried wounds was a severe burn I received as a child. While writing this book, I began experiencing sharp stabbing pain in the area of the upper arm where muscle was missing from that burn. The stabbing pain was only happening in the middle of my sleep.

*Healer Wisdom *is out of print and was replaced by* Emotional Patterns.

When I was four, my grandmother knocked a hot iron off the ironing board onto my right arm. The burn destroyed muscle tissue in the lower part of my forearm and the middle of my upper arm. The burn left only minor scarring on my upper arm, even though the burn extended between the loss of muscle tissue in my forearm and upper arm.

Before starting the Remen Q̄ work on the non-peace held in my upper arm, I had a knowing that I should use the Ancestral Remen Q̄ Method. The Ancestral Remen Q̄ method uses a strand of DNA as the image of the origin. I have detailed the Ancestral Method below in the exercise that begins with the pain in my arm. An in-depth explanation of the Ancestral Remen Q̄ Method is in The Remen Q̄ Method book.

Session

Breathe into presence

After breathing into presence, my left arm became very heavy and achy. I moved my awareness to my left arm and asked what was held there to create the ache. I heard "the mirror to the right arm pain." At that moment, the right arm started experiencing sharp stabbing pain. I then moved my awareness to the right arm and asked, "What is held in my right arm that is causing the stabbing pain?" I heard, "An ancestral wound of anger, hatred and branding." When I checked with my inner wisdom, the branding was an ancestral enslavement. My heart beat very fast at that moment, and I felt hot.

The Ancestral Remen Q̄ Process

> **Step 1.** Say in your inner voice with eyes closed: *I am witness to the field of intention to neutralize this field of information* (you continue to hold an awareness of the non-peace you are experiencing).

> **Step 2.** Say in your inner voice with eyes closed: *I am witness to the origins of this created pattern in the field of information*. Then, visualize a DNA strand.

> **Step 3.** Say in your inner voice with eyes closed: *I am witness to the neutralization of this created pattern in the field of information*. Then, create a shift in the visualization. Change the DNA strand into an image of your choice (sparkles, bubbles, glitter, pink dripping wax, dancing unicorns, a color, etc.).

> **Step 4. Snap** your eyes open halfway through the changing the imagery. Then, focus your awareness on your body with your eyes closed. Watch any sensations as they arise in your body. Stay focused on the sensations in your body until they are complete.

1) First Ancestral Remen Q̄ process: When I witnessed the DNA strand, a bright light, similar to a star, appeared on the DNA strand. As I witnessed the neutralization process, the star appeared to get big (the change), like a dying star, and disappeared. As I write this, a sense of peace comes over my body.

    Body Check-In: A pulse sensation in the mirroring left upper arm has transitioned to feeling swollen. The right arm feels as if life force is flowing into the forearm. When I move my awareness to the scar, I see an intense red glow and my left forearm aches. The mirroring left forearm feels a band of constriction around the upper arm, and the image of an iron band appears in my inner vision.

2) Second Ancestral Remen $\bar{Q}$ process: When I witnessed the DNA strand at the beginning of the process, a small light appeared on the DNA strand. The light appeared to be very far away. At the neutralization stage, the small light disappeared.

   Body check-in: The band of constriction felt on the left arm is now a spot. The right forearm now has a deep muscle ache. The red glow of the scar is now black.

3) Third Ancestral Remen $\bar{Q}$ process: When I witnessed the DNA strand at the beginning of the process, a small light appeared on the DNA strand. The light appeared close to me. At the neutralization stage, the small light left the DNA strand, spiraled like a firework, and disappeared.

   Body check-in: The energy of the scar appears much smaller now, with a spot of black. The spot of constriction on the mirroring left arm is gone.

   At this point, my intuition tells me I need to switch to the basic Remen $\bar{Q}$ process.

4) Fourth Remen $\bar{Q}$ process using the basic Remen $\bar{Q}$ process: I witnessed violence in the origin stage of the process.

   Body check-in: Arms are 80% improved and feel lighter. My awareness of the scar is now a tiny black spot.

   There is a sense of expansion in my body.

5) **Fifth Remen $\bar{Q}$ process using the basic Remen $\bar{Q}$ process:** I witnessed a little girl fleeing violence.

   Body check-in: Arms feel good and lighter. The black dot has gone.

Result: A sense of calm and peace.

Additional Notes: The colors I saw in the scar represented the emotional wounding I held there. I interpreted the red as representing anger, and the black represented hatred.

Part II: Metaphysical Exploration of the Third Eye Chakra

Chapter 7: The Third Eye

Many spiritual traditions connect the third eye chakra to intuition and spiritual awakening. **This chakra holds the attributes of intuition, creative thought, mindfulness and insight.** If the third eye chakra is impaired, then you may experience a feeling of being stuck, lost, can't receive, disconnected, and confused.

The pineal gland* is the physical manifestation of the third eye chakra in many spiritual traditions. The pineal gland senses light and dark. But as you will see in the Appendices, the pineal gland does much more. The gland has color receptors inside and a lens on it for receiving light.[14]

In some spiritual traditions, the third eye is associated with the pineal and pituitary glands. Other traditions reference only the pituitary gland; conversely, some only reference the pineal gland. I will explore the pituitary gland in upcoming writings.

The third eye chakra is part of the subtle energy body. Chakras, auras, and nadis (energy channels for life force energy) are part of the subtle energy body.* Similar to physical body aspects, a chakra can become congested or contracted. When a chakra is congested or contracted, there is a corresponding disharmony and imbalance in the physical body, possibly resulting in disease. As we journey to inner peace, we work to transmute the fears, created patterns and emotional states that cause congestion and contraction in our subtle, emotional, physical and mental bodies. Transmuting the limiting patterns in the third eye chakra and the pineal gland, using energetic activation techniques and a detoxing routine, will move you toward wellness and balanced activation of your intuition. **

See Glossary pages 115 (aura), 116 (chakras), and 121 (nadis) for more information.

***Yoga, meditation, inner reflection, herbs, Reiki, sound healing, essential oils, Remen Q̄ and more all support the transmutation of physical, energetic and emotional limitations affecting the third eye.*

---

[14] Arendt J, Aulinas A.(2022) *Physiology of the Pineal Gland and Melatonin*. In: Feingold KR, Anawalt B, Blackman MR, et al., editors. Endotext [Internet]. South Dartmouth (MA): MDText.com, Inc.; 2000-. Available from https://www.ncbi.nlm.nih.gov/books/NBK550972/

An over-activated third eye may create out-of-balance "intuitive or psychic" information. Intuitive, uncontrolled information is fear-based, may make you sick, and represents an out-of-balance third eye chakra. The third eye begins to activate when you place your awareness in that space.* But that activation is constrained by emotional wounding. This wounding shows up in your pineal gland and intuition. When intuitive information is uncontrolled, it is like drinking from a fire hose, except instead of going into your lungs and choking you, the flood of energy overwhelms your body. When I observed this flood of energy in others, they appeared overwhelmed to the point where they had trouble functioning in everyday life. They experienced vertigo, insomnia, headaches, fatigue and a rapid heartbeat. Intuitive information coming through that filter will be colored by overwhelm. This type of information has poor boundaries and may disrupt the flow of your life. Often, this out-of-balance information is given unrequested to others. I call this psychic diarrhea.

You can also activate the third eye by tapping the center of the forehead or use an activation balm. There are probably several other methods of third eye activation, but unless you have transmuted the wounding held in the pineal gland and third eye, those methods will be short-lived.

A congested third eye chakra does not allow intuitive information to flow. You do not look to your inner wisdom for clarity. There is a feeling of being stuck and confused. You flit from thought to thought and feel your memory is impaired. You may start overthinking and have difficulty making a decision. Overthinking will also be a diversion from the Inner Peace Journey Work. If you overthink, use that as your non-peace reference and do Remen $\bar{Q}$ until you have reached a place of calm, neutral or peace before starting any other transmutation work.*

Important: Always start with the feeling of non-peace present in the moment. Overthinking or any other trauma response is interwoven with other states of non-peace. You don't need to know the story; start with the present feeling of non-peace.

An open and activated third eye will contract when intuitive emotional wounding, detailed in the following chapters, is triggered. For example, I recently experienced a male acquaintance "man-splaining" my role in a developing situation. At first, I was amused and curious about what would come out of his mouth next. But his condescending statements triggered a long-buried wound. At first, I was annoyed, and then I compulsively took on a deluge of tasks and activities for myself. I went into overdrive and became hyperactive. I was in overwhelm. When I became aware of what had happened, I immediately felt a pressure in the center of my forehead as my third eye responded to my understanding.

The image below has a highlighted area between the eyebrows, where a slight pressure may be felt during third eye chakra activation. When looking at this image, you may feel a pressure or a tingling in the center of your forehead.

The third-eye chakra is the **gateway or portal to higher levels of consciousness**. It is the link between the visible and invisible aspects of nature.[15] It is a different level of knowing. This level of knowing gives insight into our true nature. Your perception and insight broaden as you transmute the fears and limiting patterns restricting the third eye. You better understand your inner self as the third eye functions more fully.

You have a knowing beyond the surface. Information from the third eye chakra opens you to consider the ramifications of your actions. You will know the probable outcome if you take a specific action. Once you know that potential outcome, you might consider taking a different path, as the outcome may not be peace.

For example, a neighbor puts her dog outside during the daytime while she is at work. The dog fears being in the backyard by itself and barks for 8-10 hours a day. This dog's barking disrupts the peace and annoys the neighbors at home during the day. Since I am at my computer at least 8 hours a day, the barking began to wear away my tolerance and erode my peace. Many neighbors complained to the dog owner. The dog owner seemed to ignore their complaints. I reflected on my options. Complaining did not seem to work. The next level was starting the process of filing a dog nui-

---

[15] Hall, Manly P (2015 pp. 4) The Pineal Gland: The Eye of God, Comprising Chapter XVI of Manly Hall's *Man: The Grand Symbol of the Mysteries*. Martino Publishing, CT

sance complaint. I could send the woman a bark collar, which gives a shock when the dog barks. None of these options felt peaceful or correct. I then decided to see if Remen $\overline{Q}$ 'ing the non-peace of the dogs barking would help. The dog is now barking less; at least, I don't notice or hear the dog. But recently, another shift has happened. The dog is no longer being put in the backyard to bark all day.

Accessing higher knowledge of a spiritual nature, universal wisdom, and awareness is difficult if the pineal gland is impaired. An impaired pineal gland implies a congested or contracted third eye chakra. If the pineal gland is impaired, you identify more with your physical and ego self. Therefore, your awareness focuses on the body. This over-identification with the physical may lead to excessive pleasure-seeking, reactive fear, aligning with institutional fear, addictions, focusing on survival fear, anchoring in an illness or many illnesses, etc.

When you are present in the moment and at peace, the third eye allows for clarity in decisions. With third-eye clarity, you can be aware of the whole and not just the details. Otherwise, if you are not at peace and your third eye is impaired, the creative energy for problem-solving anchors in fear. There is a focus on what you must do to be safe instead of creative problem-solving.

An expanded level of awareness will facilitate compassion for others. With an expanded awareness, you will become aware of the wounding that has created non-peace in your relationships with others. Your awareness will be of the non-peace and the wounding that created the non-peace relationship.

The pineal gland is part of the creative flow that accesses universal wisdom if you are open to receiving it. The creative flow of the writer, the artist, the mathematician, etc., is a knowing of the solution. For example, I had a complex problem in one of my programming classes in school. I met with one of the graduate students to see if I could find my way to an answer. As I entered the meeting room, I knew the solution. I didn't know the details, but I knew the result. Then, when I went to the board, I drew out the solution. With each step, I knew what was next. In my writing, I will pose a question and begin writing. The answer aligns with my higher self and is often profound.

Institutions (religious, educational, corporations, familial, and government) wound the flow of creative energy and, by default, the pineal gland. The institutions tell you that you must only use the tools they teach to create; you must stay inside the box. This implementation of problem-solving controls the creative process and, by default, you. A controlled and Wounded Creative Core* also keeps you from knowing the spiritual you. This wounding keeps you from the grace of flow. Flow is giving and receiving in balance. The Wounded Creative Core keeps you fearful of receiving and only supports giving. It also says you are sinful if you don't give. The wounding of the creative core is also a wounding of the pineal gland.

See Glossary page 123 for more information about the Wounded Creative Core.

Using your intuition allows you to know the magic of our existence. The Universe is a wondrous place with an endless supply of discoveries. With an activated and peaceful intuition, you become aware of the other realms beyond the third-dimensional awareness. You stand in the presence of a glorious sunset and realize the oneness of all. When used without impairment, intuition brings us to a place of our purpose. Without an integrated intuition, you are just going through the motions; you are an institutional zombie. For example, that glorious sunset doesn't bring you to a transcendent state; it is just a colorful sky. Or you listen to music and it's just sound; it never touches your heart. The majesty of what you are witnessing does not inspire you.

The pineal gland and the associated third-eye chakra are about flow. By allowing the intuitive knowing to flow, you are empowered and accept yourself and your inner knowing. Flow is the receiving of life. You must be able to receive before you give; otherwise, you are giving from nothing. Giving from nothing depletes you. Anything you give from that place has an emptiness to it.

As you proceed to peace, you will have spontaneous experiences of knowing as you unwind the non-peace held by the pineal gland and third-eye chakra. These flashes of intuition can feel exciting. It can also stop your spiritual growth. **Many people get stopped by being able to "know" what's hidden.** They think of themselves as unique. These episodes of intuition become an attachment to the ego, a trap. If this becomes an aspect of your identity, you have set up a spiritual bypass (see page 122 for more information). Knowing historical information or future events does not move you forward on your journey to peace.

Chapter 8: Developing Your Intuition

Developing your intuition is dependent on allowing awareness. You cannot force the third eye open; to do so is fruitless. Any emotional wounding and physical impairment would cause the forced opening to revert to its prior state. By allowing, you are not forcing but witnessing information making itself known. A balanced opening of the third eye is your natural state.

As you notice changes in your intuition, just be aware of the information and allow it to flow through. The experiences are not an identity. The activation of intuition is where someone whose intuitive centers are opening can get stuck. Intuitive experiences can seem novel and exciting at first. This phase can be a trap. You may think and feel you are something special. This feeling and thinking will keep you stuck at this stage in your journey until you understand that intuition is simply the flow of information from universal wisdom. If the information requires action, do the action with neutrality and then allow the information to flow through. Do not hang onto the information. For example, a woman joined a spiritual group. One day, she asks an intuitive question about her teacher, and the information that flows through says the teacher has egoic motives for teaching. She decides to leave the group and never looks back. She does not contact the other members and tell them what she has discovered. She uses the information she receives for her own action, growth and information. She is neutral about what she has received. If she is stuck in a phase of intuition development, then the intuitive information may come through a filter. The information may be skewed based on emotional wounds; a filter held in the third eye. Sharing the information reflects a lack of judgment and may be possibly wrong.

Another example would be a person's friend has become romantically involved with a new person. The person feels something is off with her friend's new love interest. She asks an intuitive question, and the answer confirms her feelings. In this case, her action is to be a friend who is open to being present to her friend as she navigates the experiences of this relationship. If the person is stuck, she will tell her friend what she 'knows' and possibly lose a friend.

Our intuition uses our senses to bridge between information energies and our awareness. For example, you may "see" an image in your mind's eye or "hear" your inner voice. I will smell a rose or floral fragrance when specific energies are near. I have had the experience of smelling diseases. If I have a knowing of an adverse event, I will get a contraction in my heart. That squeeze is information. These experiences conveyed information that came through my senses from the intuitive realm.

Awareness Exercises

1. You receive information through your senses, and you learn by observing it. It is through these observations that you build awareness. When you numb out or ignore information from a sense(s), you stop the flow of awareness. The heart is as much a sense as smell or taste. The heart has two states that give you information: contracted (non-peace) or peaceful (this may feel expansive, neutral or calm)

   You may have ignored a heart contraction, alerting you to possible problems. If you were present to your heart's feelings, you remember that feeling in your heart. Did you listen to your heart, or did you ignore the feeling? If you ignored the feeling, why? Journal this information and then Remen $\overline{Q}$ the response. What were other experiences of ignoring your heart? Again, journal and Remen $\overline{Q}$ the response.

2. Do a body scan* of your pineal gland. Journal what you see, feel, know, hear, etc. As you do the scan, notice if your heart contracts or you feel tension in any other part of your body. If you notice a contraction or body discomfort, Remen $\overline{Q}$ the contraction (a place of non-peace) until the contraction is a place of peace.** Rescan the pineal gland, and do Remen $\overline{Q}$ until there is peace and no contraction. Come back to this exercise periodically and note what you observe. You may find that there is more Remen $\overline{Q}$ to do.

   *If you have no experience with body scans, see the Resources section on page 124 for instructions.

   **With Remen $\overline{Q}$, you do not need to know the cause of the contraction.

   You can build your body scanning skills by scanning your body and recording your impressions. If there are states of non-peace that arise, Remen $\overline{Q}$ the non-peace until you have peace and then remember to lean-in.

3. Review the emotional patterns (fears, emotional states, and created patterns) in Chapters 9 through 11 of this book. Stop on anything that triggers a contraction in your heart or body. Journal the limiting pattern and then Remen $\overline{Q}$ the non-peace.

While reviewing the limiting patterns, you may suddenly feel exhausted, overwhelmed, sleepy, unfocused or scattered. If this happens, Remen $\bar{Q}$ the feeling as a point of non-peace until there is a feeling of peace and calm. Then, use Remen $\bar{Q}$ to transmute the limiting pattern that triggered the feelings of being ungrounded. An ungrounded feeling may take over your thinking. When that happens, use the grounding meditation on page 126. Do not reread the limiting pattern that caused you to feel ungrounded until you have Remen $\bar{Q}$'d the feeling of ungrounded. After taking back your peace, reread the limiting pattern and note how you feel in your journal; if it is still non-peace, use Remen $\bar{Q}$ until you feel peace, calm or neutral in your heart.

If the fear, emotional state or created pattern has been an ongoing issue, you may need to lean-in.* The reason for this is explained on page 8 of The Remen $\bar{Q}$ Method[16] book. Some wounds transmute wholly and quickly; others require additional rounds of Remen $\bar{Q}$. There may be many different vibrational frequencies of a limiting pattern for which you have the same label.

*See Resources page 130 for more information.

4. Do the following exercise for only a few minutes at a time. This exercise will activate your third eye. Meditate on the third eye. Bring your awareness to your third eye. Notice its color. Notice the feeling you get in the meditation. Is there a sound? What's the texture? Hold the awareness of your third eye and imagine breathing into and out of the third eye. If non-peace arises, use Remen $\bar{Q}$ to bring you to peace. After the Remen $\bar{Q}$ exercise, move your awareness back to the third eye and repeat the meditation. Has the color changed? Are you experiencing any other bodily sensations? I suggest journaling this information. Journaling will give you a baseline against which you can become aware of changes. As this meditation exercise evolves, aspects of limiting beliefs or wounds will arise in your awareness. Take the time to write them down and then use the Remen $\bar{Q}$ to transmute these contractions to peace.

---

[16] Moore, Valeria (2021). *The Remen $\bar{Q}$ Method: An Easy Do It Yourself Process to Create Inner Peace and Change Your Reality.* Keizer, Oregon, USA; Three Moons Publishing

Develop Calmness

Develop a sense of calmness when using your intuition. When developing your intuition, calmness is an essential state for your mind. To achieve a calm mind, I suggest you practice meditation daily and do your Inner Peace Journey work. Additionally, sitting for a moment and watching your breath until you can feel a shift in your awareness may be helpful before engaging in intuitive work. The inner work, using Remen $\overline{Q}$, moves you to a sense of peace. When you sit to meditate, looping thoughts or worries can sabotage your meditation session. Use Remen $\overline{Q}$ to transmute the worries or looping thoughts.

You can perceive the ripples if you throw a pebble into a still pond. If you throw a pebble into a pond that is in upheaval, you will not be able to perceive the ripples made by the pebbles.

Boundaries

The most painful lesson I had to learn was boundaries around what I allowed to enter my awareness. As a young girl, I just learned to keep my mouth shut. I did not share what I perceived from intuitive information. I always felt like I was saying the wrong thing if I did say anything. Many years later, I would take a class that would change my life: Perceptive Awareness Technique. This class taught me a process for accessing my intuition. In effect, it puts guardrails around the flow of information. I can tell the difference between my thinking mind information, intuitive information received without asking and intuitive information I receive through an intentional process.

If you receive information, you did not ask for and it is helpful, then ask if this is true, compassionate and accurate using the Intuitive Question Process on the next page. Additionally, ask a question that would give you the same information if accurate. Generally, this process is used intentionally to access intuitive information.

Intuitive Question Process

1. Breathe into presence (see page 25)

2. Visualize a dodecahedron* in your mind's eye, in front of you and above your eyes. With your eyes closed, raise your eyes as if you were seeing a physical object with your eyes open.

   Note: The dodecahedron is one of the Platonic solids. The visualization of Platonic solids will facilitate the opening of intuitive information pathways. Plato associated the dodecahedron with the ether or elements of heaven. Once the intuitive pathways have been established, you can stop using the dodecahedron visualization.

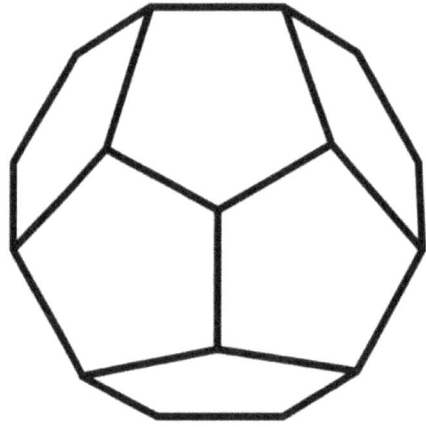
Dodecahedron

3. Repeat in your inner voice. "I intend that my heart-soul wisdom (see Glossary page 120) activate true and accurate information for me now."

4. Ask your question in your inner voice. "I intend to know the accurate, true and clear answer to this question." State your question. Record your answer.

Discernment

In the early 2000s, I attended a gathering. I thought this was simply a gathering of like-minded folk to connect. At that time, I was very naïve about the metaphysical world and always interested in learning. As the gathering progressed, we went into a large room and sat in an auditorium setting. To my surprise, a woman unknown to me started channeling. She was taking everyone into a trance. I did not know what was happening, but everything in me fought going into a trance. My senses were telling me this was wrong. This woman then crossed many boundaries and told another woman to get her affairs in order and that she would die soon. I left that gathering as soon as I could get out of there. This story is an example of boundaries crossed in a potentially harmful way.

Discernment is about using our intuitive skills in a way that does not harm others. Discernment is an **insight** into "right" or "wrong." The energy of discernment moves inward. It is not judgment. Judgment implies power and is outward in its impact. If I were doing a body scan reading, I would share seeing different colored energies or energies that appeared congested or devitalized. I had one reading that I was not even aware I did. I stared at a mole on a fellow student's arm (I had no memory of this). I never said a word to this student. Later, I discovered that my staring so perturbed the student they went to the doctor. The mole was cancerous and caught in time. There was a higher level of awareness in action there.

Due to trauma, you can lose your ability to discern when you hold limiting patterns of feeling unloved and unwanted. You become a people pleaser and do what you think will make you special, wanted, loved, approved and accepted.

Ask yourself the following questions and use Remen $\bar{Q}$ to transmute to peace (remember to lean-in) if the answer is one of non-peace.

1. Can you ask questions of others and feel safe? Do you feel afraid when you ask questions?
2. Do you receive intuitive information that shames you? Do you experience being shamed by others? Does receiving intuitive information feel shameful?

3. Do you receive intuitive information about someone and then tell them about it without permission? If you are itching to share, transmute the feeling of non-peace. Ask yourself, "What about this information applies to me?" and "Why do I need to feel special?"
4. Does intuitive information offer you neutral insight that is information? Or is it judgmental, divisive or illogical?
5. When giving and receiving intuitive information, can you walk away from information and remain neutral about the outcome?
6. Does intuitive information frighten you?
7. Do you find yourself in situations where you feel pressured to make a decision?
8. Can you feel your heart tell you when something isn't right? Or do you ignore the messages you are getting? If you ignore your heart's messages, why?
9. Do you trust your judgment?
10. Do you feel safe making decisions?
11. Do you know what it feels like to make a decision and feel centered in peace?
12. Do you easily get manipulated by others?
13. Do you take responsibility for your actions, or do you blame others?
14. Do you espouse your intuitive gifts to others to seem special?
15. Does intuitive information offer insight or demand you "see?"
16. When you receive intuitive insight, does it feel uplifting and gentle? Or is there an extreme feeling to it? When writing the emotional patterns, I get a feeling of discovery and joy.
17. Do you fear a psychic attack? If you fear a psychic attack, then there is a relationship you are holding that brings in that energy. This fear tracks to a limiting emotional pattern(s), disease or an ancestral influence. Remen $\bar{Q}$ the fear of a psychic attack. If you are so inclined, develop a mantra, for example, "I am guided, protected and loved."

Some of the questions below may pertain to intuitive people in your sphere or yourself. We tend to gravitate to like-minded groups and people where we feel safe. The need to be in the company of people we feel safe with may override our intuition. We may find ourselves in the company of intuitives who filter information through their wounding when utilizing their intuitive skills. This wounding may take the form of intuitives using information for power, monetary gain and fulfilling their need for acceptance. Use Remen $\bar{Q}$ to transmute to peace (remember to lean-in) if the answer is one of non-peace. Journal your impressions and the information that arises from these questions.

1. Do you feel pressured to make choices that are not good for you? If so, do you feel comfortable saying no? Are you placed in group situations where you are subject to groupthink? Groupthink is the practice of making decisions as a group in a way that discourages dissent or individual responsibility.
2. Do spiritual teachers or leaders in your sphere espouse their specialness and channel information that you did not request? Are these people crossing boundaries to assert their power or control? Or show that they are special? Do they have another agenda, such as making money from you? Are they always right? Can they be questioned without accusing you of a betrayal or persecuting them?
3. Do you belong to a group(s) or institution that demands unequivocal loyalty or worship? The leader/teacher is always right? Are you empowered to direct your life? Or must you allow others in the institution to direct your life? Does the leader/teacher encourage you to betray others or lie?
4. Do you work with or learn from people who say you will only heal through them? Or are they always right? There's a justification for everything they do?
5. Do you feel powerless and helpless when around members of your spiritual community? I suggest you take back your power and Remen $\bar{Q}$ that feeling of powerlessness until you feel calm and neutral.
6. Are you free to leave the community? When you answer that question, do you feel nervous or anxious inside? If you feel a contraction in any part of your body, Remen $\bar{Q}$ that feeling of powerlessness until you feel calm and neutral.
7. Are you taught that you can access enlightenment through the teacher? Are you being taught that you are not far enough down the spiritual path to move forward without the teacher? Are personal decisions and movements being made by the teacher?

Give yourself the power of discernment by also giving yourself space. When you receive intuitive information that gets your attention, consider what the source might be. Did you ask for the information? If not, sit with the information, go into a light meditation and do the Intuitive Question Process above on page 52; ask, "What is the insight I need here?" The response should be one of compassion. If not, disconnect and transmute the relationship using Remen Q̄.*

If you do not feel capable of disconnecting from a source that feels wrong, temporarily close your intuitive flow by saying, "I am stopping my intuitive flow of information for now," and contact a trusted spiritual counselor or one of the Remen Q̄ teachers for support.

What is acceptable intuitive sharing with clients?

If you are working with a client as a medical intuitive, I suggest you not diagnose anything you might perceive while doing a body scan. I have had clients become assertive about wanting to know whether they have cancer or not, and I have been just as assertive about not answering that question. You never want to answer that question with anything other than "You need medical advice from your doctor." You can describe the energy you perceive, the color, the emotional content (beliefs, fears, or emotional states) and whether it is devitalized or congested. I have had clients who had symptoms they had been struggling with for way too long. They had not sought medical care for a variety of reasons. My advice was always to seek medical care. You can help clients with their fear of getting medical care by teaching them Remen Q̄ and guiding them through the exercises to reach a place of peace.

If you are working with a paying client as an intuitive, you have their permission to give them intuitive information. Often, a client will know the answer to their questions. They will ask questions like "Is this new boyfriend the one?" or "Will this new job be good for me?" If they ask questions, they already know the answer. They don't trust their intuition and seek someone else to give them information. You can then turn the questions around. For example, "What makes you question that your new boyfriend is the one?

When working with clients as an intuitive, you have permission to give them intuitive information, but at no time do you have permission to be unkind, harsh or demonstrate a lack of compassion. Compassion is listening without judging your clients. Compassion is a feeling of kindness toward your client. If your intuitive readings lack compassion, you may want to take a break from your intuitive work and do some Inner Peace Journey Work around being judgmental or critical of others.

Tidbit: It has been my experience that people may be attracted to a specific healer or intuitive counselor because they have a similar emotional wound. Before meeting with any client, I suggest you Remen $\bar{Q}$ any non-peace that arises before your session. You can be vague about the intention. For example, you define the non-peace as the emotional wounding you have in common with the client.

What is acceptable intuitive sharing with friends?

You may have an unspoken agreement with your friends that sharing intuitive information you perceive is OK. Respecting their boundaries by asking if sharing is OK is still a good idea. I will sometimes call the information my opinion. The information should be neutral without judgment. Being neutral means delivering the information with kindness without any added energy from your feelings.

If you receive harsh information and there is no way to rephrase it, I will ask my friend questions. It's been my experience that they already know the information you have received. For example, "Is my husband cheating on me?" or "Am I going to be laid off"?

Sometimes, my inner voice will pipe up with additional information. If the information clarifies a person's earlier conversation, ask if they would like my opinion. If that information is harsh and asking questions is not working, you may want to go back and ask your intuition if there is a more compassionate way to present information if it is needed. You may want to isolate yourself and ask the question again. I have found that the answers will always come with space, time, and sometimes at 2 a.m.

If I feel that a friend is ill, I may ask if they are feeling OK or make a statement that they appear pale or flushed (I may perceive auric color changes). These are all friendly observations of caring that may be part of friendly discourse.

Helpful Hints

1. As your third eye opens, you may become hyper-aware of your other senses. Sounds may seem loud and annoying, light, colors or smells are overwhelming, etc. You may need to alter your environment to be more comfortable. If that is not possible, use Remen $\bar{Q}$ to move to peace in the moment and do a grounding exercise. The hyper-sensory experiences will be the place of non-peace for the Remen $\bar{Q}$ exercise.

2. Just as you may have a hyper-sensory awareness, you may also experience emotions as being excessive or "over the top." The same advice applies, Remen $\bar{Q}$, the non-peace that arises until you feel calm and at peace.

3. If, after working through the exercises, making a practice of journaling, removing pollutants and Inner Peace Journey Work to activate your third eye, you still feel that your third eye is blocked or out of balance, then you may be holding patterns of belief that keep the third eye from functioning. These beliefs may be epigenetic. Use the ancestral method below.

Ancestral Remen $\bar{Q}$ Process

To use the ancestral Remen $\bar{Q}$ process, breathe into presence using the method given at the beginning of this section.

Step 1. *Say in your inner voice with eyes closed:* ***I am witness to the field of intention to neutralize this field of information*** *(you continue to hold an awareness of the non-peace you are experiencing).*

Step 2. *Say in your inner voice with eyes closed:* ***I am witness to the origins of this created pattern in the field of information.*** *Then, visualize a DNA strand.*

Step 3. *Say in your inner voice with eyes closed:* ***I am witness to the neutralization of this created pattern in the field of information.*** *Then, create a shift in the visualization. Change the DNA strand into* *an image of your choice (sparkles, bubbles, pink dripping wax, dancing unicorns, a color, etc.).*

Step 4. Snap *your eyes open halfway through, changing the imagery. Then, focus your awareness on your body. Watch any sensations as they arise in your body. Stay focused on the sensations in your body until they are complete.*

4. If you are struggling with your intuition, the following practices may help.

    ✦ Meditate. When you meditate, you are not trying to control the outcome; you are allowing the flow of information. Meditation is also helpful for stress. Stress blocks intuition.

    ✦ Pay attention to your first thoughts and information that flows into your mind as you awaken. Observing your first thoughts is a way to become familiar with the flow of your third eye. For example, while writing this material one morning, I experienced an awareness that I needed to transfer money to my checking account. About 30 minutes later, a request came from a loved one needing a short-term loan. She had an emergency and needed help quickly. While writing this book, I would ask myself, "What should I write today?" Sometimes, the message was "Take the day off" or "You need to work on the introduction."

    ✦ Journal daily. Ask yourself, "How have the institutions (religious, corporate, family, community, and education) created beliefs, limiting patterns and or fears restricting me?" Journal the thoughts that arise, then use Remen Q̄ to transmute those limiting states to peace.

    ✦ Seek an experienced breathwork teacher to guide you through the process. Breathwork can facilitate intuition by helping to calm the mind and body. When the mind and body are calm, it is easier to access intuition. Breathwork can also help to increase awareness of the body and its sensations. This process can help to make it easier to notice subtle signs of intuition, such as a gut feeling or a sudden insight.

+ Seek out a yoga, Tai Chi, or Qigong class. A foundation of these practices is an awareness of your body. The movements require focus on positional awareness; you are ever present to the signals your body is sending. Body awareness and sensing what your body is telling you is intuition. For example, the back of my neck will tense up, and my heart will contract when I am in a space that is not safe.

+ Engaging in creative activities like art, music, writing, or dance can help bypass the logical mind and tap into the intuitive and subconscious realms. Creative expression can unlock insights and enhance intuitive abilities.

+ Practice energetic hygiene by taking a daily bath or shower.

+ Practice mastery of thoughts. Suppose looping thoughts are an issue. Remen $\overline{Q}$ the subject, non-peace, of the looping until the looping stops. If worry is an issue, Remen $\overline{Q}$ the subject of the worry. Remember to lean-in.

+ Read, reflect, and study works by spiritual masters, such as Buddha, Master Choa Kok Sui, Robert A. Johnson, Valerie V. Hunt, Rumi, Paramahansa Yogananda, Kahlil Gibran, Krishnamurti, etc. This list is only a minuscule portion of the reading I have done. Let your intuition be your guide. Go to an actual brick-and-mortar bookstore or library and peruse the shelves in the metaphysical or personal development section. Set an intention that the book you need will be made apparent. Be aware of your body's feelings as you read through the titles. What you need to know at that moment of your Inner Peace Journey will create desire when you encounter the book you are to take home. There is a possibility that the book you are drawn to is outside of your comfort zone. For example, you may be drawn to a book on witchcraft or an esoteric book of writings. There is something you are being called to learn within those pages.

Chapter 9: The Stages of Intuition Development

Everyone is born with intuitive capabilities. As your intuition awakens, you become aware of this source of information, your sixth sense. Some people move through the opening of the third eye at a graduated pace that mirrors their emotional, mental, spiritual and social development. Others may become stuck at a particular phase of intuitive development due to emotional wounding, or they may have set up a spiritual bypass.* Getting stuck will pause your journey to inner peace and limit your spiritual growth.

See Glossary page 122 for more information.

Your third eye awakening or opening is integral to your spiritual development. At each phase of intuition development, you will grow into a new level of awareness, knowing that comes through the third eye. Each new level of awareness brings in a greater sense of compassion for others and yourself.

Intuition is not seeing the future; the future is many different possibilities. Attempting to use intuition to see the future blocks the flow of inner information and guidance.

When I started exploring the different stages of intuition development, I became aware of four stages. I then had a vision of the following stages:

- In a cave with a stick
- Stick becomes a wand
- Wand becomes nightmares
- Nightmares become illusion

Each one of the phrases above represented a stage. At each stage, you develop the wisdom to transition to the next stage of development. In the first stage, there is complete darkness in the cave with a stick (intuition) and nothing else. Intuition (the stick) facilitates your **survival**. Like the stick in the darkness telling you there is a jutting rock or if you have just poked a bear, intuition at this phase tells you if there is danger. Intuition development advances to the next stage unless wounding has paused development. Once you have transmuted this wounding, you become aware of a new level of knowing. The next stage is **creation, where** the stick(intuition) becomes a wand. The intuition wand creates magic. If you develop an identity connected to the creations from this stage, you start **dancing with the ego**. The **dance with ego** will eventually take you to your shadow(nightmares). At this stage, you either transmute your shadow and move into **self-realization** (understanding that everything is an illusion and the sixth sense is a tool for traversing the illusion) or pause until your identity no longer claims ownership of the creation. As you **dance with the ego,** you will move back and forth between the first three stages of development.

This chapter explores the following at each stage of intuition development:

- A more detailed look at the stages of intuition development.
- How do you know you are stuck at a stage of intuition development?
- The emotional patterns if you are stuck at a stage of intuition development.
- Possible physical ailments if you are stuck at a stage of intuition development.

Survival Stage

In a cave with a stick

- You are born with this level of intuition activated.
- Intuitive information comes in the form of hunches and guesses
- Intuition informs your feeling of safety. You get a feeling that something is wrong.
- You feel you need psychic protection from psychic attacks.
- The creative core* is wounded by conforming and complying.

The creative core is that aspect of our being that embodies and brings creativity into the world (see Glossary page 116).

In a cave without illumination, the stick is reaching out for information; is there a wall, a rock on the floor in front of me, etc.? The stick is your intuition; knowing flows through the filters of survival. As you use the stick, you only know how this information impacts your safety. You do not know what you have encountered. You do not know the color, actual size, or what it is.

During this stage, you are unaware there is intuition (the stick). A child will use their empathy to survive an abusive childhood. The wounding of an abusive childhood has caused the child to become a wounded empath. At this stage, the child, as a wounded empath, experiences the feelings of others and makes them their own. They will also take on the guilt, shame, worry, etc. of these feelings. The wounded empath may move between the survival and creation stages of intuition development until they have transmuted the childhood wounds.

As a child, I was unaware of my intuition, but it kept me from harm several times. Growing up in a dysfunctional and abusive household, I developed into a wounded empath. My empathic abilities kept me from harm as I became aware of the changes in the adults around me. In my late teens, I found myself in several situations that would have resulted in severe bodily harm, and at least one would have resulted in my death had I not used my intuitive abilities.

The Wounded Empath[17]

How do you know if you're a wounded empath?

You may be a wounded empath if you answer yes to any of the questions below.

- Do you sense other people's feelings and make them your own?
- Do you think that you are responsible for other people's feelings?
- Do you feel guilty if someone is angry, sad, or upset?
- If your boss or domestic partner appears upset, do you immediately think, 'What did I do wrong'?
- Do you feel exhausted and drained of energy most of the time?
- Do you suddenly feel like you are on the verge of tears for no apparent reason?
- Can you say how you feel and feel safe?
- Do you get frequent colds, sinus infections or other viral infections?
- Do you have trouble turning down extra work or community volunteer requests? Do you feel your energy and time stretched to the breaking point? Do you feel like you have no time for self-care?
- Do you suffer from burnout?
- Do you struggle with stress and depression?
- Do you have trouble letting go of a hurt or something that went wrong? Do you continually replay the situation in your thinking?
- Do you perceive the world through a filter of 'What did I do wrong'?
- Do you frequently feel hopeless and feel that life will never improve?
- Do you try never to rock the boat (cause controversy) and make others happy?

One of the intuitive abilities that we are born with is our empathic sense. The empathic sense allows us to sense the emotions and feelings of others. Those feelings may encompass physical feelings as well as emotional ones. The empathic sense sends physical feelings to the body, interpreted within the framework of other intuitive senses and beliefs. For

---

[17] Moore, V. (2018). Wounding of the Empathic Sense. Available from
https://emotionalpatterns.com/wounding-of-the-empathic-sense/

example, you meet a friend for a coffee date. You see this friend frequently, so you are familiar with their energy and moods. During the coffee date, you get a feeling that something is off. The friend seems slower than usual and a bit distracted. As an empath, you sense your friend's change in your body. Your heart may feel contracted, and there is concern that something is wrong, although your friend has said nothing. The concern is felt in your heart, and your intuitive knowing senses that something is bothering your friend.

If the intuitive senses hold wounding, the empathic information received from the intuitive senses will come through that wounding. For example, I "knew" when my parents were angry as a child. I could feel their anger even if I had not seen them. My heart and tummy would immediately clench. Their anger may have been at each other, but I interpreted it as my fault. I believed I would be hurt when a parent or any other person in authority was angry. I would focus all my energy on surviving until their anger had dissolved. I would ignore all other information that may have flowed through the intuitive senses.

The self-realized empath has developed a response to empathic feelings that acknowledges feelings and their source. This response knows that these feelings are not theirs but empathic information. They see their empathic sense as the catalyst for a compassionate response as inner peace in the face of suffering.

The empath, who is **dancing with ego***, experiences the feelings of others and takes responsibility for someone's physical pain, anger, disappointment, failure, etc. This empathic sense developed as a finely honed survival skill in response to a threatening environment. The energies of others may cause a psychically sensitive person to feel physical and emotional pain.

See page 82 for more information.

The empathic sense becomes wounded when a child is sensitive to the stimuli in their environment. Anger, depression, sadness, and loud voices by anyone will terrify a sensitive child. The reaction is a wounding of the empathic sense. The sensitive child takes the energy of these emotions and believes it is their fault the adult is unhappy.

The sensitive child may feel lost in a household with many children and chaos. They may not feel there is a safe place to be themselves. The chaotic energy of a large household can wound the empathic sense. The child goes unrecognized and begins to believe that all they do is wrong.

A healer with poor boundaries due to a wounded empathic nature can find themselves energetically drained at the end of a day of working with others. These poor boundaries may also contribute to misunderstanding psychic information. This person can lose track of their own needs in the face of working to meet the perceived needs of others. The empath's unmet needs color the filter through which they receive information. This healer is attached to the outcome. In a few years/months, they will burn out.

In my teens, I worked as a nurse's aide and studied to be a nurse. Being psychically sensitive[18] made working in a hospital emotionally, psychically and physically overwhelming. I grew up in the Bible Belt*, and there was never a discussion of intuitive abilities. I did not know such a thing existed. That would have been considered 'devil talk' and the cause for receiving a severe 'talking to' and hundreds of hours of prayer.

The Bible Belt is the Southeastern area and one Midwestern state of the United States where the Christian Bible is held as being literally true. Christianity plays a major role in day-to-day life, and people tend to have conservative views.

When I started working as an intuitive, my "gift" was knowing the suffering of others. I would start a client session and immediately begin to feel the pain they were experiencing. It might be a headache, nausea, foot pain, or residual pain from a significant accident. I would sense the emotions they held that had led to the disease or lingering pain. I had very poor boundaries, psychic and otherwise. I did not know how to access the information in a structured approach (to ask the right questions); I didn't even know that was an option. I allowed psychic information to affect me when working with others. My rationale was that I was helping people, which may have been true, but I burned out in a few years.

I didn't realize what I was doing to myself. I thought that was the way it was supposed to be. I was doing transformation work to help people. But I was a wounded empath, taking on everyone's feelings and thoughts.

---

[18] Dale, C. (2011 pp. 15). The Intuition Guidebook. Minneapolis, MN: BRIO Press.

When I reached my wall, I stopped everything for several years. That break brought me back into balance. During that hiatus, I journaled my thoughts, studied, and developed Remen Q̄. Using Remen Q̄, I transmuted the need to be a people pleaser and be everything to everyone. That change allowed me to access the flow of information with discernment.

Possible Physical Issues of the Wounded Empath*

- Constant stomach pain or nausea when they are powerless to leave a situation, such as an underage child might feel.
- Sexual organ dysfunction
- Pancreatic issues (diabetes, pancreatic insufficiency, etc.)
- Depression
- Entity attachment
- Constriction/tightness in the chest
- Headache/migraines
- Back/shoulder dysfunction
- Low self-esteem
- Sleep issues/Professor Mind (can't shut thoughts off)
- Liver enzymes are out of balance
- Lower jaw teeth (broken, cavities, root canals)

This is not a definitive list.

Emotional Patterns for the Wounded Empath

Emotional States

- ❖ Hide in the middle - This could be likened to hiding in plain sight. A person with a wounded empathic sense makes decisions based on not creating controversy or comment. They adjust what they say and do to stay safe. They stay safe by making sure they have pleased the people around them. They have spent so much time in this place they have lost touch with their authentic self. They no longer know what they believe or feel. They have taken on the beliefs of others to be safe. Their own needs are suppressed. They may find that when they have taken on too much of the energies of others, they start to cry. If the person is asked why they cry, they will not know. They just know that they have a deep inner sadness.

- ❖ Can't say no -They cannot say 'no.' They take on more and more responsibility or tasks because if they say 'no,' they may hurt someone's feelings or make someone angry. They believe they will be hurt if they hurt someone's feelings or make someone angry. They work very hard to please others. To them, an angry person is dangerous. They work to avoid confrontation with others.

- ❖ Always a feeling of being in trouble -There is a nagging feeling in their chest or stomach that they have done something wrong and are about to get into trouble. This feeling is with them all the time. They have a constant feeling of living on the edge of disaster. They carry a projection that everything that goes wrong is their fault.

- ❖ Sexual feelings are confused for love - Love-based relationships confuse sexual feelings and feelings of love from the heart. They commit quickly to relationships with no fundamental understanding of the other person. They have come into the relationship with a distrust of their intuition, so they don't trust that level of information. The closeness brought about by a sexual relationship becomes their basis for love. This basis for love, in time, often leads to disillusionment. When the relationship fails, or they can't seem to do enough to please the other person, they have just received validation that their feelings are dangerous and can't be trusted. This results in the creative aspect being denied or shut down.

- ❖ Masculine and Feminine are out of balance - The feminine aspect is strong and reflects an overactive anticipation of the needs of others. The masculine is weak, and the person doubts themselves. They are sure they will fail and fear putting themselves out there.

- ❖ Skewed sense of appropriate social reactions - The family may have had drama queens/kings who were dominant in the family structure: mother, father, grandparents, etc. They dominated the conversation and energy in the household with their physical/emotional needs. The family dynamics led to no one else being allowed to safely express their physical or emotional feelings. The expression of feelings was met with ridicule or shame. The empath learned early in life that it was risky to express their feelings. They also learned not to trust what they were feeling. Their feelings became a source of self-betrayal that would lead them to ridicule or shame. Intuition is not trusted and is suppressed. The empath may not know how to appropriately communicate their feelings of physical or emotional discomfort. For example, an empath may laugh at a friend's explanation of a recent misfortune or freeze when confronted with someone's grief. The ability to react appropriately to someone else's physical or emotional discomfort has become dampened and may not be appropriate.

- ❖ Always in a state of analysis - The mind of a person with a wounded empathic sense is constantly searching for the right answer, the right thing to say, and the appropriate reaction to external events. Their responses must be based on a logical thought process, not feelings. An analytical sequence of thought must back everything up. If they are wrong, there is no shame in a faulty logic process. The shame is felt if their response is based on feelings. If they make a mistake, they will go back over every step in the sequence until they know precisely where the error occurred.

- ❖ Sense of being alone - This person is in constant inner turmoil. They have a feeling of being alone and that no one understands them. They have no inner peace.

- ❖ They make decisions they know are best for them but suffer deep regret and guilt for those decisions.

Fears

- ✦ Fears feeling bad
- ✦ Fears other people's feelings
- ✦ Fear of knowing too much
- ✦ Fear that they won't know in time
- ✦ Fear of harm/hurt
- ✦ Fear of being seen
- ✦ Fear of making waves
- ✦ Fear of being diminished
- ✦ Fears angering others
- ✦ Fears of not fitting in
- ✦ Fears upsetting people

- ✦ Fears being asked to do something
- ✦ Fears confrontation
- ✦ Fears doing something wrong
- ✦ Fear of saying something wrong
- ✦ Fears their feeling
- ✦ Fear of failing
- ✦ Fear of trusting self
- ✦ Fear of being wrong
- ✦ Fear of being alone
- ✦ Fear of being out of control
- ✦ Fears being overwhelmed
- ✦ Fear of disapproval
- ✦ Fear of showing their feelings
- ✦ Fear of not being loved
- ✦ Fear of saying the wrong thing
- ✦ Fear of being shamed
- ✦ Fear of disappointing others

Created Patterns

- Bad things happen when I'm not looking.
- Crying is for babies.
- Everything is my fault.
- I am always wrong.
- I am powerless.
- I am bad.
- I am worthless.
- I am depressed.
- I am guilty of everything.
- I am in trouble.
- I am responsible for all bad things that happen.
- I am responsible for everything.
- I am alone.
- I am shameful.
- I am to blame for everything.
- I am to blame when things go wrong.
- I can never let my guard down.
- I can't speak my truth and be safe.

- I can't let go of _____.
- I can't make a decision unless I have all the facts.
- I can't paint/write/draw/_____(creative efforts).
- I can't say no.
- I can't shut my brain off.
- I can't speak my truth and be safe.
- I can't trust my family/people.
- I can't trust my mother/father/brother/sister.
- I don't know what it feels like to say no.
- I don't know god's definition of compassion.
- I don't know god's definition of love.
- I don't know god's definition of my authentic self.
- I don't know how to feel.
- I don't know how to feel safe in my body.
- I don't know how to say no.
- I don't know how to trust my feelings.
- I don't know the difference between my feelings and someone else's.
- I don't know what it feels like to trust my feelings.
- I don't know what love feels like.
- I don't know who I am.
- I don't trust myself.
- I don't understand the difference between sexual feelings and love.
- I don't/can't trust my feelings.
- I must always be on alert.
- I must analyze everything before making a decision.
- I must do what others want me to do.
- I must take care of everyone else first.
- I feel guilty when I do something good for myself.
- I always regret doing what is best for me.
- People make me feel guilty for taking care of myself.
- I must be quiet to be safe.
- I must take care of others to be loved/wanted/accepted.
- I must tell myself what to feel.
- I need permission to feel.
- I want to die.
- I will never be good enough.
- I'm no good at creative things.

- I'm not good enough.
- I'm not loved.
- If I relax, someone will hurt me.
- It is not safe to be in my body.
- It is safer to be analytical.
- It is weak to feel.
- Listening to my inner voice is dangerous/wrong.
- Love is pain/hurtful.
- My feelings are irrelevant.
- My feelings are wrong.
- No one will believe me if I tell them how I feel.
- No one will believe me if I tell them the truth.
- Others tell me what to feel.
- People are mean.
- People hurt me.
- People think I am lying.
- No one understands me.
- I don't deserve peace.
- I need approval to be safe.
- I don't know what inner peace is.[19]

Helpful Exercises for the Wounded Empath

While working through the emotional patterns of the wounded empath, you may want to adopt an energetic hygiene to remove and transmute the energies you pick up. The following are some processes I have learned that I have found helpful. I have learned these techniques from an array of teachers and friends.

1. If you are an emotional release practitioner (see Glossary page 117), I suggest you use Remen $\bar{Q}$ to transmute the emotional wounding you hold that resonates with your client. It is 'common' healing lore that you attract clients who hold similar emotional limiting patterns. When using Remen $\bar{Q}$ you don't need to know what limiting pattern

---

[19] Moore, V. (2018). Wounding of the Empathic Sense. Available from
　　　https://emotionalpatterns.com/wounding-of-the-empathic-sense/

you share with your client. You set the intention for peace with an awareness that you have a common limiting pattern(s). By doing this, you have created a neutral space for working with your client.

2. At the end of the day, take a shower. Water is an excellent cleanser of energies you have picked up. Some have found that a quarter cup of sea salt in a bath is preferred. I have also discovered a wonderful addition to your shower. There are essential oil-imbued bath salts that come in cubes called shower steamers. You place one in the bottom of your shower, and it releases the essential oils into the shower steam.

3. Stand barefoot on the ground and imagine the energies you have collected from the day flowing into the ground. Earth energies will transmute and purify devitalized energies. This process is also known as Earthing.

4. If you are a bodyworker, you can do one of the following between clients:
    a. Place your palms together, one hand on top of the other with the fingers pointing in opposite directions, and rub the palms together briskly at least three times. Then, break from the rubbing quickly by pulling your hands apart.

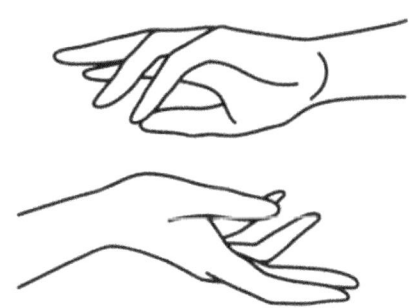

    b. A technique I learned in Pranic Healing: Imagine an orange flame on the floor. Using your hand in a slight cup with fingers together, sweep the opposite arm and hand just above the surface from shoulder to fingertips. At the end of each sweeping stroke, flick your fingers at the end of the sweep as if you are flicking something into the imaginary orange flame. After you have done the opposite arm, imagine the flame disappearing.

Alternatively, use a half-full bucket of water mixed with one cup of sea salt instead of the orange flame. When you have finished, put the saltwater in the toilet.

I perceive the energy of sea salt to be an orange color. Orange is the color of purification and transmutation of energies.

c. Prepare a spray bottle with vodka in it. After working with a client, spray your arms and hands with the vodka (I learned this in Pranic Healing, also). Vodka* has no odor and will evaporate quickly.

The energetic color of vodka is peach colored, a paler version of orange.

d. If you have the option, stand in the sunshine for 5-10 minutes (this may not always be possible) and take several deep cleansing breaths, imagining air prana going out into your body from your lungs.

Creation Stage

Stick becomes a wand.

- The spiritual fire of passion has been lit.
- Synchronicities
- Your awareness takes you into the divine.
- Flashes of insight and inspiration
- Lack of control and discernment with information received intuitively
- You are bringing in information within the context of your wounding
- You are still making choices based on fear
- Your journey to self-realized intuition is beginning
- The quality of information changes from survival information to insights about the people and events touching your life.
- There is a loss of objectivity; you cannot detach from your visions.

At this stage, you begin to be aware of the magic of the sixth sense. Synchronicities begin to happen. You think something, and it happens. You think of an old friend, and they call. There are flashes of insight or awareness. This stage feels like your intuitive sense is magic as you adjust to this stage of awareness. You may feel a sense of mystery and awe at this new level of awareness.

The feeling of magic can become a trap that will stop your spiritual growth. At this stage, there is a tendency to get lost in magical thinking*. You live for the next vision, the next past life regression**, or the next psychic or tarot reading. You are living in the magical thinking of a spiritual bypass*** that will stop your Inner Peace Journey. The intuitive information received at this stage is mundane.

See Glossary page 121 for more information about magical thinking.

**See Glossary page 121 for more information about past life regression.*

***See Glossary page 122 for more information about spiritual bypasses.*

The need to know spiritual information was a driving force for me during this phase. I spent thousands of dollars on books and workshops. This quest sought spiritual wisdom. I would reflect on what I had learned in those books and workshops. The reflection would often bring me to my shadow. My Inner Peace Journey work at this stage became healing the emotional wounds I held and searching for a way to do that healing. The wisdom was all within me. As I entered this phase, I was still a wounded empath, moving between survival, creation, and dancing with the ego stages of intuitive development.

I shared what was happening to me with a small group of friends. Some friends thought they could use my new abilities to their advantage. A friend approached me at a party and wanted to know what the stock market would do. I enjoyed the attention I received, and my ego embraced the new identity emerging with my growing intuitive and healing art skills. Other friends became distant and disappeared from my life, and others reflected my low self-esteem and self-worth. This change triggered many life changes as I moved toward a purpose I did not yet consciously know.

How do you know if you have set up a spiritual bypass?

- Do you consult the 'cards,' a pendulum, use muscle testing or a psychic to make **many or all of your** decisions?*

*When you use tools or other people to inform your life journey, you are not transmuting the wounds, activating and developing your intuitive skills. One of the critical elements of this journey is **ownership and trusting** yourself. The use of these tools becomes a spiritual bypass. However, besides the fact that they create a spiritual bypass, they may also be inaccurate.*

The use of a pendulum moves you away from accessing your higher wisdom. You rely on a tool instead of trusting your inner voice or knowing. Pendulum use is not always accurate. According to the training I received, using a pendulum is based on your mind state at the time of use. I have found that the results from using a pendulum are no better than random chance. Others have found that the pendulum is highly accurate for them.

Muscle testing is based on the idea that your muscles will either strengthen or weaken when a statement is made. The muscles are tested for strength when a statement is made to determine its truth to you. One method is that your forefinger and thumb are pressed together, and a healing practitioner holds your fore-

finger with one hand and the thumb with the other hand. As you make a statement, the healing practitioner will easily pull your fingers apart if the statement is false. Or, using both hands, you make interlocking circles with your thumb and forefinger pressed together; when a statement is made, you pull the fingers apart and break the circles. The supposition is that your muscles will weaken, and your fingers will pull apart easily if the statement is false. The problem is that fingers can develop diseases that weaken them, for example, arthritis. If your blood chemistry is out of balance, the muscle testing will be incorrect. If you are dehydrated, the muscle test will be inaccurate. If you are emotionally distraught, the muscle testing will be incorrect. Additionally, I have experienced people forcing the results of the test. Several scientific studies have evaluated the validity of muscle testing, and the results indicated that muscle testing was no better than random chance.[20,21]

One of the reviewers of this book was upset that I was taking away their tools for "knowing." I am not taking away anything. You decide whether using these tools is advancing your Inner Peace Journey or stopping you from doing the inner work needed to heal your intuition. If you are not using your inner wisdom to make decisions, you have stopped your Inner Peace Journey.

Further insight about muscle testing can be gained by reading <u>Power vs. Truth: Peering Behind the Teachings of David R. Hawkins</u> by Scott Jeffrey.[22]

- Do you get intuitive information in a flash of insight and loop on that incident for days?

- Do you handle problems with magical thinking*? For example, instead of getting a job or building a business and doing the work, you believe that by "pulling" a few beliefs and repeating a few affirmations, your money issues will disappear.

*See Glossary page 121 for more information.

---

[20] Staehle, H. J., Koch, M. J., & Pioch, T. (2005). Double-blind Study on Materials Testing with Applied Kinesiology. *Journal of Dental Research*, *84*(11), 1066–1069. Available from https://doi.org/10.1177/154405910508401119

[21] Unproven Diagnostic Tests. (n.d.). FoodAllergy.Org. Available from https://www.foodallergy.org/resources/unproven-diagnostic-tests

[22] Jeffrey, S. (2013). *Power vs. Truth: Peering Behind the Teachings of David R. Hawkins*. Creative Crayon.

Another example is when you use affirmations, like "I am wanted" or "I am loveable," without doing the work of transmuting the created patterns and fears around feeling unwanted and unlovable. Every time you repeat the affirmation "I am loveable," your body, heart and mind will react. You have triggered your wounding. You are not healing yourself; you are re-wounding yourself.

- Do you take responsibility for your health by getting the appropriate medical care, or do you rely on a psychic reading to determine medical treatment? Do you "pull" a belief and think your heart disease (or any other medical problem) will go away? *

Sometimes, a physical problem will go away instantly. I have had that experience. But, if this is a severe problem, is the belief change simply masking the need for medical care, creating a bypass?

- Do you get enamored with the next shiny object in the metaphysical world? Do you believe the new shiny object will take you to the next level of spiritual growth? (Shiny objects would be a new book, a new spiritual guru/teacher, a new healing art modality, a new crystal, a new energy technology for healing, a new energy tool, etc.)

- Do you look for the easy way or a shortcut through difficult emotional issues?

- Do you blame others for putting negativity out in the universe? Or create the potential for someone to feel shame by telling them they have created their reality.

- Do you spend money on manifesting courses? Do you think you can solve all your problems through a manifesting course?

- Do you present yourself at a higher spiritual level than others?

You probably set up a spiritual bypass if you answered yes to any prior questions.

Possible Physical Issues of the Creation Stage*

- Congestive Heart Failure and other heart diseases
- Impaired fertility
- Lower Right Jaw (temporomandibular joint dysfunction, gum disease, broken teeth, dental cavities)
- Non-Alcoholic fatty liver disease
- Reduced immunity
- Autoimmune disease
- Asthma
- Bronchitis

This list is not definitive.

Emotional Patterns for the Spiritual Bypass

Emotional States

- ❖ Short-winded -- knowledge of their being was constrained and held until they could breathe again. (Clarification: This means holding their breath in a frozen state.) Fearful of the next thing to happen, they hide and freeze in mythology (their story). The mythology gives them cover so they are not seen.

- ❖ Wrongly led by another in charge, they find themselves confused and overwhelmed by the principle presented. Instead of questioning and challenging, they hide in their submission and conformity.

- ❖ Definition of life met them in a field (their identity), a desert of knowing (clarification: nothing was there). They felt **lost and ungrounded**. They looked for wisdom in all the wrong places (following a false teacher). Their knowing was unknown – nothing. They feared confrontation and a challenge to their wisdom (in their heart, they knew that their "wisdom" was self-serving and stopped their inner peace journey).

- ❖ They were left alone with no foundation, no voice, and no direction. No one stood by them. No one was there to cheer them in a direction, aimless and lost.

- ❖ They have knowledge, but it is no more than a saying or platitude. The words are hollow and plastic. Plastic words crumble. They sweep them up and look for more plastic words to replace those that turned to dust. They fear real words. Real words would lead them to their pain.

Fears

- ✦ Fear of breathing
- ✦ Fear of living
- ✦ Fear of knowing
- ✦ Fear of the secrets
- ✦ Fear of being a witness to the pain of others
- ✦ Fear of feeling compassion
- ✦ Fear of witnessing suffering
- ✦ Fear of losing their story
- ✦ Fear of being present
- ✦ Fear of being alone
- ✦ Fear of being lost
- ✦ Fear of being abandoned
- ✦ Fear of being wrong
- ✦ Fear of confrontation
- ✦ Fear of being the odd one
- ✦ Fear of being different
- ✦ Fear of change
- ✦ Fear of flow
- ✦ Fear of being vulnerable
- ✦ Fear of being heard breathing
- ✦ Fear of standing up
- ✦ Fear of being their authentic self
- ✦ Fear of being true to self

Created Patterns

- I'm not good enough.
- As long as I don't breathe, I am safe.
- If I breathe, they will know how to find me.
- If they find me, I will be hurt.

- Knowing is dangerous.
- I will be hurt if I know the secrets.
- I can't have joy and be safe.
- I can't have peace.
- Secrets are dangerous.
- I can't stop them from hurting others.
- Compassion hurts.
- Compassion will get me hurt.
- If I see others being hurt, I may get hurt also.
- When things change, bad things happen.
- I will be abandoned, shamed, and destroyed if I am different.
- Confrontation is dangerous.
- I must hide and be invisible to be safe.
- My story keeps me safe.
- My story is my identity.
- I must do what others tell me to do.
- If I am wrong, I will be humiliated.
- I am lost.
- I don't trust my inner voice.
- I don't trust my inner truth.
- I can't face hard truths.
- I must ignore the truth to be safe.
- If I see the truth, I will be an outcast and lose my community.
- I am depressed.
- I am angry.

Dancing with the Ego

Wand becomes nightmares

- Ego creates an identity from intuition.
- Spiritual growth may be paused.
- Lives from judgment: right, wrong, good, bad.
- Looks for validation from others.
- Beginning to understand and develop discernment with information received intuitively
- Transmutation (doing the shadow work) of the limiting patterns that filter intuition has begun.
- You are developing and calling upon your intuition skills for guidance.
- Your intuitive senses will begin to balance with information flowing from multiple clairs (*see page 90*).

At this stage, you are **dancing with the ego. Dancing with ego** is a process of transmutation. Working in the shadow can take you back into the **survival** and **creation** stages; it is a dance. The forward and backward movement into and out of the intuition stages brings awareness to the limiting pattern filters. Your work with Remen $\overline{Q}$ at this stage transmutes the limiting patterns of your shadow and elevates the quality of intuitive information. In this stage, we learn to master our intuition skills; this is a form of spiritual mastery. We develop self-trust by transmuting the wounds that impact our intuitive self and refining our intuition skills. The transmutation work within this stage is developing neutrality about the information you receive. When you are neutral, you upgrade the quality of the information flowing through you.

During this phase, I moved between **survival**, **creation** and **dancing with the ego**. I had unusual and disconcerting experiences of past lives and unexpected insights. I had begun my shadow work.

I vacationed in New Orleans with my partner in the 1980s. I had never been to New Orleans. As we entered the French Quarter, a wave of knowing and strange desires entered my awareness. I "knew" where to get a good bowl of jambalaya and gumbo and how to get there. I had to have a long woolen cape and a particular type of lace handkerchief, and I "knew" where the shop that sold them was. I "knew" what was around every corner. My voice began to change. I was unnerved by my familiarity with a place I had never been. New Orleans was just the beginning of synchronicities and past life experiences I would have over the coming years.

This past life experience created an opening in my thinking. I began to expand my spiritual reading. I started engaging in spiritual retreats. I began to notice the synchronicities. That trip began a cascade of events that, over the years, would propel me through many life changes.

On a trip to England in the 1980s, I wanted to experience many places, including Hyde Park. Once I got to Hyde Park, I found many artists displaying their paintings. One painting drew me in. The painting was hanging on a fence, approximately 3 feet X 4 feet in size. It was not a great piece of art, but the subject matter triggered a feeling of knowing and not knowing. It was a painting of a castle on the bank of a river. There was a boat sailing around the turn in the river. The atmosphere was a mystical, foggy evening with an air of intrigue. I **had** to have that painting. I did not ask about the name of this castle, where it was located, or even if it was real. I was about to embark on a train and bus trip across Europe, and hauling around a rolled-up canvas would be inconvenient. But I had to have the painting. I then carried that rolled-up canvas on my trip across Europe.

I was sitting at my desk in 2022, and a new digital wallpaper appeared that day on my computer. It was the castle in my painting. I now had a name, the castle of Almoural in Portugal. This castle was a bastion of the Knights Templar. Control of the castle was transferred to the Portugal Knights Templar master in 1129 A.D. I had not connected the castle image to a past life until it appeared on my desktop. This past life brought the understanding that the path to inner peace is a lifetime process of transmutation, study, and reflection.

The many past life memories that occurred in the following years were not just a reminder. These memories taught me that we are multidimensional beings. They also taught me that the fascination with past lives can be a spiritual bypass, the shiny object that diverts your attention and can stop you from progressing in your spiritual development. I learned that when one of these past lives surfaced, I had to stop and ask what I needed to learn or know about my journey in this lifetime and then allow it to drift back into the divine spiral of the time continuum. Sometimes, the message might take 30+ years to be delivered.

How do you know if you are stuck in the Dancing with the Ego Stage?

- Do you have difficulty listening to your inner wisdom and using the information yourself?
- Have you immersed yourself in your shadow work and felt as if it was endless instead of feeling joy at the progress you have made?
- Do you need others to recognize your intuitive skills or healing art abilities?
- Do you identify the value of people, things, events, etc., in the field of duality (right/wrong, good/bad)?
- Do you see the same clients over and over that have mundane questions? For example: Is this relationship going to last? Do they love me? Will I get this job? Should I hire this plumber?
- Did you take on an identity that has stopped your Inner Peace Journey?

Possible Physical Issues of being stuck in the Dancing with the Ego Stage*

- Arthritis
- Foot problems
- Knee problems
- Chronic Kidney Disease
- Muscle spasms
- Upper respiratory problems (colds, flu, bronchitis, asthma)
- Seasonal allergies
- Depression
- Blood diseases (anemia, hemochromatosis, etc.)
- Digestive diseases (Gastro-Intestinal Reflux Disease, Ulcers, Crohn's Disease, etc.)
- Diabetes complications
- Heightened sense of pain in your body
- Diseases that result from being anchored to one spot for too long

This is not a definitive list.

Emotional Patterns for Being Stuck Dancing with Ego

Emotional States

- ❖ Bad decisions brought them to a place without a foundation, ungrounded. They are without understanding for others. False information led them astray into a world without boundaries, discipline, or self-control. Meaningless conversations caused them to learn that they were adrift and needed to attach themselves to something (In their transition to this stage they may be looking for a place of belonging, a community. This will give them a platform from which to build their identity and it also a place where they can become stuck for a while), or they would become invisible and disappear (fear of becoming invisible and not belonging).

- ❖ Falseness permeated their life. They knew little of why they were doing what they were doing – they felt lost. Building their profile of magic created an identity with no basis. They look to others to find meaning.

- ❖ Short-sighted – don't see that they are stuck in a place of magic that is a field of diversion with no purpose. Don't know how to be anything other than what they are now and feels locked into that path—tunnel vision. Financially, it feels like there are no other options. They resist the urge to stop dancing with the ego. (This is where they are being prompted to leave this stage and move forward on the Inner Peace Journey. But this stage offers financial security. So, there is a pull of ego and the pull of the heart.)

- ❖ False ideas lead them to believe they are at the rainbow's end. There is nothing else in this journey. They feel that where they are at is the realized self. They cannot loosen their grip (an attachment) on their 'way' in the world. There's a safety in the world they have built. They are looking for rest and predictability.

- ❖ They have stopped the Inner Peace Journey. They feel fatigued with life. There is a feeling of being battered and abused by the long and intense nature of their journey. They want to stay where they are and BE. Build a solid identity at this stage so they feel like they at least know that much.

Fears

- ✦ Fear of living
- ✦ Fear of life
- ✦ Fear of disappearing
- ✦ Fear of being invisible
- ✦ Fear of being wrong
- ✦ Fear of being responsible
- ✦ Fear of being in your body and feeling
- ✦ Fear of compassion and knowing
- ✦ Fear of being grounded
- ✦ Fear of being seen
- ✦ Fear of not having a purpose
- ✦ Fear of having a purpose
- ✦ Fear of having an obligation
- ✦ Fear of being lost
- ✦ Fear of change
- ✦ Fear of listening to their inner voice
- ✦ Fear of moving
- ✦ Fear of emotional pain
- ✦ Fear of hurting
- ✦ Fear of the nothingness
- ✦ Fear of being nothing
- ✦ Fear that they will not have strength for the rest of the trip
- ✦ Fear of not knowing

Created Patterns

- My life is just smoke and mirrors.
- I am nobody.
- I am invisible.
- If I make a decision, I will be wrong.
- If I am wrong, I will become nothing.
- If I don't know the answers, I will be shamed.
- I can't face my wounding.
- I must hide my wounding.
- I am nothing.
- Change is dangerous.
- If I stay still, I will be OK.

- I am lost and cannot find my purpose.
- I have no purpose.
- If I am seen, I will be hurt.
- I lose myself if I am compassionate.
- Being in my body will only get me pain.
- If I am wrong, I will be hurt.
- I can't trust my inner voice.
- I need others to keep me from disappearing.
- I find my meaning through others.
- I need my magic to be seen.

Self-Realization

Nightmares become illusion

- Creation is inspired
- Divine guidance is consciously accessed
- You realize that the flow of your life is no longer your choice
- You are neutral to the intuitive information
- You trust the information that is received
- Information is soul-focused and multi-dimensional
- You open to multi-dimensional compassion

At this stage, you realize the interconnectedness of the universe. Nothing is separate; everything connects to everything. A knowing of the universe emerges. This knowing comes softly and quietly. You begin to 'see' multiple paths for relationship dynamics. Your responses are conscious choices and non-reactive. There is a knowing of the outcome of your choices. The shadow (limiting patterns) has been transmuted to peace as part of the Inner Peace Journey Work.

I am currently in a state of becoming. I am beginning to see visions from many years ago come true. Those visions reflect a new way for the world. Those visions were of death to an old way of being and giving birth to something new. My emotions are in a compassionate, neutral state. There is only being present to the next thing waiting.

In 2009, I traveled to Chartres to study Alchemy. Upon my return, I had several dreams that reflected the spiritual transformations that were underway. The first dream was of a man killing his wife and child in an elevator that was going up. An interpretation of this dream would be that there was a completion of one phase on the journey of spiritual transformation. On that same night, I dreamed of being pregnant. The pregnancy meant I was pregnant with that next level of spiritual transformation. The two dreams brought messages of birth and death, a new beginning and completion. Then, a dream followed of a lone bird in the sky flying. The lone bird suddenly split and became hundreds of birds flying in different directions. I interpreted that dream to mean that my spiritual awareness would affect many others.

Chapter 10: The Clairs

Our intuitive senses are called clairs. The word 'clair' is French for clear. Clairs are fields of awareness, coupled with physiological receptors, that flow information from the universal mind. Each clair uniquely conveys information. The clairs defined in this chapter are clairvoyance, clairsentience, clairaudient, claircognizance, clairempathy, clairalience, clairtangency, and clairgustance. Sometimes, multiple clairs receive multiple information streams. For example, your inner voice tells you information, you have a knowing, and simultaneously, you are experiencing imagery of that information. The following is a descriptive list of the different types of clairs:

- **Clairvoyance** is 'seeing' hidden information. Clairvoyance may be seeing the moment, possible future, or past events. Sometimes, the seeing takes the form of vignettes, symbols, sounds, colors, or a vision. Clairvoyant information of the future will be the most probable outcome of many possibilities.

- **Clairsentience** is a feeling you get in your body, usually in response to a situation. You may refer to it as a 'gut' feeling. Clairsentience could be your whole body or a sensation in your heart region. You may experience sensing or feeling of disease, thoughts, or emotions of others.

- **Claircognizance** is a knowing. You may have a "knowing" of danger or the potential for harm. You don't know what the danger is, but you have a knowing of impending harm. When evaluating a statement's truth, you may know whether it is truthful or false. You may get the answers to questions without any objective data; you have a knowing.

- **Clairalience** (also known as clairessence or clairscent) is the ability to smell and discern information about what you are smelling. Some people experience the vibration of disease through smell. They have learned that each disease has a unique smell. Diabetes will smell different from lung cancer to someone with an awakened and informed intuitive sense of clairalience. This sense may also manifest as smelling the emotions or feelings of another.

- **Clairaudience** is hearing voices beyond the human hearing sense. This sense can take the form of hearing the thoughts of someone close to you. You experience hearing an inner voice warn you of an upcoming difficulty. Clairaudience may be experienced by hearing the voices or sounds of the past in an area.

- **Clairempathy** is the ability to sense the emotions or feelings of another.

- **Clairtangency (psychometry)** is the ability to feel, see, hear, and know information by touching an object. Objects hold the vibration, the energetic signature of a person that has touched the object.

- **Clairgustance** is the experience of tasting energetic information. You may experience taste sensations that do not correlate with food or drink.

Clair Wounding

Emotional wounding due to intuitive abilities can reduce a clair's ability to flow information. Open clairs are part of a balanced, healthy body. If you have emotional imbalances that affect your clair(s), they will also affect your body. For example, you have a knowing of something that will happen. You share that knowing with a friend, and they ridicule you or chastise you. You may feel humiliated, attacked, and shut down the use of that skill or no longer share your insights. The shutting down of the flow of universal wisdom may serve institutional control, but it does not serve universal unity. This reduction of universal wisdom restricts the flow of life force; it is a state of non-peace. Shutting down your clair(s) because of being humiliated and attacked could translate into diabetes, thymus, parathyroid, thyroid, or autoimmune disorders.

A clair will be wounded when there is a withdrawal of love or acceptance. An adult chastises a child after they say something that forces the adult to confront an uncomfortable truth. The child then feels unloved and unwanted. An adult tells them they do not know what they are talking about and humiliates them. The child may be sent away from the adult as punishment. For a child, receiving information through a clair is a transparent process. They do not yet filter. They only start filtering and shutting down clair information when they fear the ramifications of saying what they know or observe. In this case, they may also reduce their conversations with adults to avoid rejection and feeling unloved. Shutting down interaction may result in the onset of throat, vocal cord, immune system, and lymph gland maladies.

Some intuitives learn early in life that they must hide their clair skills to stay safe. They suppress the sharing of universal wisdom and lie about the source of information. Being unable to be your authentic self becomes a life of quiet desperation and loss of identity. In time, this quiet desperation may become a diseased heart or a contracted and painful digestive system. The life force does not flow, evident in relationships and career decisions; they are stagnant. You learn to turn clair information into a language others can hear that keeps you safe. You may leave out more specific information so the wisdom and you will be safe. I would take clair information and then wrap it in logic. I would often research what I had learned until I had been able to get confirmation. I did not trust that I would be safe with friends or family until I had done this.

Any adult who grew up in a home with violence, alcoholism, drug addiction or mental health issues has the skill of clairempathy. This clair was essential to their survival. They detected the feelings and state of the alcoholic, drug addict, or mentally unstable adult and their co-dependents to stay safe. They adopt a role, an identity and a way of being based on what would keep them safe. The Adult Child of Alcoholics (ACOA) will have fragile boundaries. An ACOA may develop pancreatic diseases, autoimmune disorders, lung diseases, skin issues, and bone/joint disorders.

A clairvoyant sense may show you possible future events or what happened in the past. Given many potential outcomes, a vision of future events predicts the most likely outcome. If you share clairvoyant information about the future, you share a possibility. Sharing clairvoyant information about the future may bring judgment or ridicule if your information is incorrect and ignored if it is correct. You may learn not to trust yourself. You may begin to not listen to your inner knowing. You may feel judged, betrayed, diminished, and rejected. These feelings create emotional patterns that bring more experiences of being judged, betrayed, diminished, and rejected.

If one of your ancestors had clair senses that brought them punishment, you might have been born with the epigenetics* of that past trauma. That past emotional trauma may have been exile, ridicule, humiliation, excommunication, rejection, etc. This ancestor may have also endured physical torture, hardship, and possible death at the behest of religious leaders, local government, and community for possessing a clair sense. For example, an ancestor may have learned to be very good at determining which herbs would facilitate the healing of a sickness. The ancestor learned this skill from another ancestor and developed their 'knowing' of the healing properties of a plant. The head of a local church decided the ancestor was doing the devil's work. This ancestor was then possibly beaten and killed. At the very least, the community would have banished them for being perceived as evil. This event would have had a chilling effect on their family. The relatives would have been viewed with suspicion by the community. They would have had to shun that family member and part of their identity to stay in the community. They may have had no choice but to leave the community themselves. Descendants would have carried an epigenetic change from the trauma of this event. You may become fearful of anyone expressing intuitive wisdom. You may develop an intense aversion to religions and more.

See the Glossary page 119 for more information.

When you feel forced to abandon your intuitive senses, you feel lost. You will then grieve the loss. The intuitive senses are a part of your authentic self and sense of empowerment. Grief may be depression, anger, self-betrayal, hatred of community/family, or blame. These emotional states of non-peace will eventually become physical maladies.

People use the word psychic as a form of ridicule. I remember often telling someone what has happened or might happen (no safety filters yet), and I would hear back, 'What are you psychic?' or 'How do you know that?' or 'Can you prove that?' These comments belittled and invalidated my knowledge. I was not good enough to 'know.'

Many different energetic methods teach how to open and clear intuitive centers. Some of these methods are a band-aid, a temporary fix that can lead to discomfort. There may be layers of wounding that will result in the shutting down of the clair again and triggering the emotional wound. **The transmutation of your emotional wounds to achieve peace will bring the clair back to normal functioning.**

Chapter 11: The Wounded Intuitive

Your intuitive senses are a natural part of who you are. We are born with our intuitive senses open and functioning. Most institutional structures (education, family, government, corporations, scientific, religious, etc.) do not value or respect intuition. **You may experience emotional and physical wounding as a result of your intuition.** At eighteen, I experienced an intuitive vision that resulted in trauma, and I "lost consciousness." At that moment, I lost all my memories before I was 16. Later, I learned I experienced amnesia from 'seeing' the truth behind the trauma. Shortly after that event, I began experiencing debilitating migraines. I was guided to meditation by psychotherapists as a possible tool for reducing my migraines. While the meditation released me from debilitating migraines over many years of practice, it gradually re-opened my intuitive centers and allowed bits of my memories to return. The migraines were caused by the tension created by the demands of two worlds and holding a dark secret. In one world, information was from structured, sanctioned institutional sources and intuitive information was deemed worthless. The other world was creative, in the flow of life, intuitive and trusting of self. Being pulled in two different directions also created imbalances in my body's left and right sides, creating physical maladies and limiting emotional patterns.

You may 'know' something is unsuitable for you, but you suppress that knowing and do what is against your best interest to maintain institutional relationships. For example, the doctor tells you that you must use a drug for marginally high cholesterol. You '**know**' this drug is wrong for you, yet you relent and take the drug. Some medical clinics have policies rejecting you as a patient if you do not adhere to their physician's orders. One year later, you have developed a secondary malady from the cholesterol drug for which there is no cure, and it requires you to take another costly drug for the rest of your life. In this scenario, some of the limiting patterns are:

- Not trusting yourself
- Afraid to stand up to authority
- Not good enough
- Defensive and feeling judged

- Afraid of being judged
- Fear of being overrun
- Powerlessness
- Keeping hurtful secrets
- Unable to defend yourself
- Don't know what is best for you
- Fear of being rejected and punished
- Feeling worthless
- 'Knowing' is wrong
- Can't make decisions
- All your decisions are wrong

These limiting patterns did not start with the medical incident; they started as a child, possibly epigenetic or ancestral. Religious, cultural, educational, government, and family institutions from birth laid the foundation for this wounding. Our institutions have worked very hard to keep the use of intuition out of their institutions; they insist on you conforming and complying. **Intuition does not conform or comply with institutional rules.**

Religious institutions may dictate your clothing, marriage rules, gender roles, the length of a woman's hair, the use of your money, what you can say or not say, who you can love, and more. Early Christian education makes it clear you are evil and talking to the devil if you are intuitive. They would tell you that your destiny, if you were intuitive, was eternal damnation. You learned not to ask questions or volunteer information. **You may have adopted false piety and become adept at quoting scripture to stay safe.** Religious dogma has created severe punishments for anyone with intuition. Our ability to communicate directly with "the sacred" was stripped away by the Roman Catholic Church. The gnosis, wisdom of the spiritual mysteries, that was studied and revered was an aggregate of intuited information that was acquired through "listening" and ancient teachings. Gnostic movements encouraged the development of intuition. The Roman Catholic Church then went about killing all of the Gnostics or at least as many as they could identify. Being intuitive during the Holy Roman Inquisition resulted in a torturous death. When burning an intuitive at the stake fell out of favor, the institutions resorted to shame, humiliation, rejection and ridicule. Today, if you demonstrate intuition, you are labeled weird or the black sheep and possibly shunned.

Educational institutions reflect the values of the local religious and family cultures. Schools are all about the rules. Learning is rule-based. Play is rule-based. How well you do in school is based on whether you follow the rules. Recently, schools in some states have shut down libraries because books open your thinking and cause out-of-box thinking. **Out-of-the-box thinking is dangerous to institutions that insist on conforming and complying**.

Many technology companies use employee monitoring programs. Employees refer to it as "The Algorithm." You get a score that reflects your conform and comply behavior. Raises, promotions, new assignments or terminations rely on the score. Many large corporations around the world use this type of software. The message is clear: you must conform and comply or be unemployed.

As an intuitive, you learned to escape the chaos of conflicting information received from the adults around you and the intuitive information you 'knew' by shutting down your authentic self. You learned to feel guilt and shame knowing you were going to hell. You learned that you must keep your knowing secret. You learned you were not good enough. You learned there was something wrong with you. You learned to quiet the inner voice, not trust yourself, discount the inner imagery, and ignore the 'knowing.' You learned to watch those around you and mimic their behavior so none would know your secret. You silently grieved the loss of your identity.

Symptoms of a Wounded Intuitive

- Lack of creativity
- Have difficulty problem-solving
- Don't trust yourself and don't trust perceived intuition
- Mental and or emotional instability – emotionally reactive
- Difficulty grasping higher concepts of consciousness
- Locked into rigid and unbending values and thoughts
- Believes everyone else is wrong
- Difficulty seeing the forest for the trees (the big picture)
- Negative thinking
- Won't let go of old concepts that do not serve the greater good

- Over-identification with the physical – leads to addictions, obesity, over-identification with possessions
- Difficulty receiving and giving
- Low self-esteem
- Creates overwhelm

Emotional Patterns: The Wounded Intuitive

Emotional States

❖ A nightmare from the past (ancestral) has regressed spiritual or consciousness growth. It is meant to be a warning from another time that evolving beyond those around you will not be met with open arms – a warning that they will be met with ridicule, shame, guilt, exile and called sinful. (Nightmares may have involved crowds.)

❖ Use and abuse. Clair senses have been used in a way that impairs spiritual growth. Example: The clair skills are developing, and instead of using them to guide the learning and healing of themselves and others, they use them to allow others to abandon their responsibility and ownership and create spiritual bypasses. (They use their clair skills to allow others to evade facing difficult emotions and experiences. For example doing an intuitive reading that gives them "answers" instead of direction and compassion to evolve their personal growth. They don't turn the responsibility and ownership for information back to the student, client or friend.

Another example is a woman who comes to them as a client. She wants to know if her husband is cheating on her. The Intuitive reader answers "yes" instead of directing the woman back to herself and guiding her back to answers that begin the journey of transmuting the wounds around trust, abandonment, and betrayal.)

- Judged wrong by others. Information available from the clair senses has been judged wrong before the truth is known. Feeling judged shuts down further clair flow until illness takes you to a healing.

- Listening wrongly; clair information is sent through an institutional filter (religion, education, culture, etc.) that impairs the purity and clarity of the message of a more expansive awareness. This will create a lack of trust and distort the wisdom to the point where it is no longer of any value or help; it is the objective of institutions to destroy any information not sanctioned by the institution. (Our expanded awareness is meant to provide information that opens us to that next level of understanding. That next level of understanding allows us to transform states of non-peace. Understanding brings us to wisdom and peace.)

- Harsh light brought to bear on their life creates fear of exposure – diminishing them. They hide to stay safe. Use of their clair sense would bring attention and further diminishment.

- They are called to address their boundaries from their woundedness. They are tasked with the responsibility and ownership of their non-peace, their wounding. They may create distractions and suppress their knowingness to keep themselves in a *numb state*.

    Note of explanation: They developed boundaries for protection when they were young. By the time they begin to understand their intuitive skills, they have developed boundaries that hide their intuitive abilities; those boundaries hurt them in the long run. Boundaries of any kind have the long-term effect of constricting life force. Their intuitive skills guide them to knowing they created their boundaries and wounding. They have to own what they have created. This non-peace may manifest as hiding and defensiveness to keep people away and feeling judged or criticized.

- They feel like the information is unreliable. They have not developed practices that focus the information. They walk away from the development of their expanded awareness senses. They choose to let others tell them what their expanded awareness has been trying to do.

- They are deemed an outcast – different from others – and they become the party entertainment. Who they are perceived to be is now a threat to others. Their awareness may make the non-peace of others apparent. They are relegated from a cohort to an oddity. They become the target of ridicule and an effort to falsify their path of consciousness.

- ❖ Hostile intentions caused the loss of the ability to filter the noise/mind chatter and intuitive information. Keeping the mind controlled by the monkey mind (The monkey mind refers to a mind that jumps from one thought to another.) keeps them from having to feel/hear/see/smell/know information from their expanded awareness. Because to get clear, they must travel through the land of their wounding. They must own what the mind chatter is working to hide.

Closing down the intuitive senses may be a survival response to an ancient prejudice of rejection, hatred, fear of association, distrust, violence, or death toward anyone with openly intuitive senses. Your ancestors' survival response was passed to subsequent generations through epigenetic changes or ancestral behavior patterns.

Fears

- Fear of being found out
- Fear of being found
- Fear of crowds
- Fear of being exposed to the crowd
- Fear of being wrong before a crowd
- Fears exposure
- Fears being vulnerable
- Fears shame
- Fears guilt
- Fears exile
- Fears being a sinner
- Fear of being killed
- Fear of being tortured
- Fear of being ridiculed
- Fear of being diminished
- Fear of rejection
- Fear of being alone
- Fear of not having enough

- Fear of financial hardship
- Fear of being wrong
- Fear of being judged
- Fears others using them
- Fear of being seen
- Fear of their infinite nature
- Fear of being boundless
- Fear of knowing more than others
- Fear of being unwanted
- Fear of being feared
- Fear of being unloved
- Fear of being misunderstood
- Fear of being overwhelmed

Created Patterns

- I am a freak.
- I am bad.
- People shun me.
- No one understands me.
- I am always wrong.
- I can't trust myself.
- I am judged.
- I am guilty of sins against nature.
- I don't belong.
- I am alone.
- I don't know who I am.
- I can't trust others.
- I will be killed if people find out.
- I am vulnerable when I am open to others.
- Whenever I speak, people hate me.
- I must be invisible to be safe.
- When I share what I know, I am shamed.
- When I share what I know, I hide.
- When I 'know,' I am beaten.
- When I let others use me, I feel wanted.
- People only love me when they want something.
- People are afraid of me.
- People use me and then leave me.

- I must use my intuitive skills to survive. (Intuition is now connected to the wound of survival)
- I must keep to myself to be safe.
- I can't be myself and be safe.
- People make fun of me.
- People reject who I am.
- I must live my life with a façade.
- If I am found out, I will be rejected.
- If I am found out, I will be shamed.
- If I am found out, I will be humiliated.
- If I am found out, I will be tortured.
- Anytime I try to go forward, I am stopped.
- You can't be different from those around you.
- You will be punished if you are different.
- You must fit in.
- Being different is dangerous.
- I don't trust my inner voice.
- I am judged.
- I am criticized.
- People ridicule me.

Blocks to Intuition

We have other limiting patterns that may affect our intuition. Their source may or may not have originated in a direct wounding of the intuition, but they block our intuition.

Emotional and Physical Patterns that Block Intuition

Physical and Emotional States

- ❖ Ungrounded. Ungrounded means not being present to the whole you.* You live in your thoughts and fantasies. There is a tendency to fall and trip frequently. The lower part of your body does not get the entire flow of life force. When there is emotional and physical discomfort, you tend to disconnect from your body so you don't have to experience the pain. You do not connect with people because that would require that you be present to give energy to the relationship. You may have trouble focusing on tasks or suddenly feel very sleepy. Being ungrounded may be a coping behavior that you experience when stressed.

    Additionally, several of the states below may also manifest as being ungrounded.

- ❖ Medicine, Chemicals or Herbs: Any substance that distorts your perception will affect your subtle, emotional, mental and physical body. The pineal gland is a gateway to higher wisdom. If the previously mentioned bodies are impaired, then the flow of information will be impaired.

- ❖ Stress and anxiety: High stress and anxiety levels can make it challenging to tune into their intuition, as our minds are preoccupied with worry and fear.

- ❖ Overthinking: When we overthink situations, we can cloud our intuition and block our ability to tap into our inner knowing. Overthinking is also a form of worry.

- ❖ Lack of self-trust: If we don't trust ourselves, we may doubt our intuition and second-guess our inner guidance, leading to blocks in our intuition.

- ❖ Lack of mindfulness: If we are not present in the moment and are distracted by our thoughts or external stimuli, we may miss subtle intuitive signals.

- ❖ External influences: External factors such as noise, people, illness or other distractions can also block our intuition.

- ❖ Lack of practice: Intuition is like a muscle that needs to be exercised. If we don't practice tuning into our intuition regularly, it may become weaker and less accessible. Journaling is a way to practice. Ask a question to your higher self and write it down. Review the answers occasionally to see what has happened since you asked your question(s). Your questions must be precise.

- ❖ Past experiences. If you have had negative experiences, it can be challenging to trust your intuition. If you have been hurt or disappointed in the past, you may be more likely to ignore your gut feelings.

- ❖ Impatience: The pineal gland has the energy of allowing flow. A higher wisdom evolves and balances our chakras as we awaken. Awakening means we have done the inner work and are developing a more profound knowledge of our inner nature. Activating the third eye chakra is a natural process resulting from deep inner transmutation work. A premature third eye chakra opening can create imbalances in the body and mind. Forcing the third eye chakra to open because you want the process to go faster creates the possibility of mental and emotional instability, headaches, sinus or vision issues. The gradual opening of the third eye chakra allows you to develop an understanding of what you are experiencing.

- ❖ Low Self-Esteem: Self-esteem is how a person thinks and talks about themselves. People with low self-esteem are critical of themselves.

They will negatively describe themselves: I'm fat, I'm stupid, I don't deserve good things, I'm not lovable, I'm not as good as my sister, I always mess up, etc. A person with low self-esteem may be chronically ill. They blame themselves when things go wrong and won't take chances. They have a feeling of being worthless. When someone pays them a compliment, they will defer to someone else or deny they did anything worth mentioning.

Fears

- ✦ Fear of trusting your intuition. You tend to second-guess yourself and ignore your intuition as you focus more on protecting yourself from potential harm. You lack the courage to follow through on your intuition. Following through on intuition can feel risky. It can feel like you are putting yourself in harm's way. Often, there is no logical reason for the information you receive, so there is no logical reason to trust the inner voice. The institutional training you have received worked to shut down your intuition. The fear of being rejected by your family, ostracized by your community, relegated to the "lunatic fringe," cast out by your religion and called evil, etc., taught you to ignore your intuition.

- ✦ Fear of trusting others. If you are ungrounded, you are unaware of your body's messages about possible harm. Those messages require awareness and sensitivity to the information your heart or gut is giving you. In an ungrounded state, you develop an alternate strategy of not trusting anyone. You have a surface façade of love and light to everyone, but there is no heart connection.

- ✦ Fear of rejection. A feeling that love is for others, not you. Suppose you didn't adhere to the rules; you would be rejected and unloved.

- ✦ Fear of humiliation/shame/ridicule. Offering an intuitive answer to a question, problem, or dilemma opens you to humiliation, shame and ridicule.

- ✦ Fear of not being good enough. This fear may be due to low self-esteem caused by being bullied, criticized, and judged. Others may have had unrealistic expectations of you, which evolved into you having unrealistic expectations of yourself. People with low self-esteem have a negative view of themselves and their abilities. The fear of not being good enough can stop you from reaching or even setting goals.

✦ Fear of having close friends. There is a fear that they will discover you are "different" and reject you. Or they use you to circumvent responsibility, and you get blamed if there is a failure.

✦ Fear of being wrong. The fear of being wrong prevents you from trusting your intuition. If you are afraid of being wrong, you may be more likely to ignore your gut feelings and do what you "think" is right, even if it doesn't feel right. This fear may be a childhood familial, religious, or educational abuse pattern where punishment resulted from not getting something right.

✦ Fear of accepting who you are. Intuition is part of a balanced human energy system. Being intuitive is your natural state. Unfortunately, institutions have instilled the fear of intuition. As the pineal gland chakra opens and activates, you may be inclined to hide your inner knowing. Hiding your inner knowing is fear. This results in you staying small and a pineal gland chakra that constricts the life force flow.

✦ Fear that you cannot change your life, so why bother? You feel like you have no control over your destiny.

✦ Fear of persecution. This fear has its roots in our ancestry. The Inquisition, the executed gnostic groups, and the witch purges became traumatic scars on human history. These acts of violence still influence us. These prejudices and violence changed us by creating epigenetic changes. The epigenetics would have then passed to the descendants. The fear and mistrust of intuition persist to this day.

✦ Fear of annihilation by the authorities: hung, burned, beheaded, disappeared, imprisoned, exiled or run out of town. This fear may have its roots in political, religious, gnostic, racial, and witch-based exterminations that are both historical and still occurring.

✦ Fear of being different or standing out. You must conform and comply. You must be the same as others to be safe. 'Different' people experience shame, humiliation, ridicule, persecution, premature death, loneliness, and excommunication. You would have to fit in and not be different to be safe. Fitting in means you must behave, think and look like your community.

- Fear of receiving. The flow associated with the pineal gland/third eye is a continuous flow of information. This flow of information is an act of receiving. Intuition can be blocked if there is a fear or reluctance to receive. The fear of receiving may be based on abusive childhood experiences or dystopian gender biases. For example, a girl's training by her parents, religion and community brainwashes her into believing that her role in life is to be subservient and give. This girl will have difficulty receiving. She may have taken on the limiting patterns of undeserving, unworthy, or not good enough. This approach is an imbalance in giving and receiving.

- Fear of the unknown. Intuition often provides us with insights and guidance outside our rational understanding. We may block ourselves from receiving intuitive messages when we fear the unknown or things we cannot explain.

- Fear of being unloved and unwanted. There could be a need to be a giver to be loved and accepted. Receiving does not create a feeling of safety for you. You 'must' give to feel safe. If you give too much, you may be doing so at the cost of your identity. Giving too much can create a feeling of being lost and disconnected.

- Fear of obligation. A gift may become a method of manipulation where there is an expectation, an obligation, of "I did this for you; now you must do this for me." Receiving becomes a trap, a type of imprisonment and control.

- Fear of freedom: If others control you, then you fear freedom. You fear being unloved and unwanted and will give up your agency to be loved and wanted. A lack of agency will significantly impair your ability to receive.

- Fear that you are too old to be intuitive. This fear is a myth. When I was in my mid-50s, I had lunch with a previous business client, and I shared with her what I was experiencing with becoming a healer and my intuition. She became distraught with me. She told me that I was too old and that shortly, my skills would quit. She validated this comment by sharing that she had come from a lineage of healers and psychics and knew what she was saying. Her experience was not my experience. A dear friend in her mid-90s is still going strong in transformational work. You are never too old to start the journey to inner peace.

+ Fear of making decisions. Making a decision may feel very unsafe. As a child, making a wrong decision resulted in punishment, criticism or judgment. Making a decision implies that you are responsible for the consequences, which could hurt you. Intuition, as a flow of information, is a form of guidance to facilitate decisions. You won't trust your intuitive guidance if you do not trust yourself to make decisions.

+ Fear of disobeying. Fear of disobeying implies you cannot receive information or direction from another source. Disobeying means you have not complied and conformed, which results in punishment.

+ Fear of family and friend condemnation. Being intuitive may be a source of shame and rejection. Recently, I had the experience of encountering an old friend. I shared with him what I was working on and the books I had written. He turned and walked away from me without another word.

Created Patterns

- I will be ridiculed for being intuitive.
- I will be shamed if I take; I must give instead.
- I will be shamed if I receive; I must give instead.
- I am numb to the pain in my heart.
- Intuition is dangerous.
- To be safe, I must check out.
- If I have many things going simultaneously, no one will bother me.
- If I am busy, I do not have to connect with people.
- I am too busy for people.
- I am too busy for relationships.
- Being responsible is dangerous.
- I must be in control, or I will be hurt.
- I am out of control.
- I don't know when someone is telling me the truth.
- I don't know when someone is lying to me.
- I am judged.

- I am guilty if bad things happen.
- I get blamed when things fall apart.
- I must stay very still and be very quiet to be safe.
- I must hide and stay very still to be safe.
- Knowing the future is bad.
- Knowing the secrets will get me killed.
- People will fear me if I know the future.
- Knowing the secrets will ruin my life.
- If I "know," I will lose everything.
- Psychics are all scammers.
- Psychics are thieves.
- People are afraid of me.
- I can't be better than my spouse/life partner.
- I don't trust myself.
- I don't trust my inner voice.
- I trust logic over my intuition.
- It is safer to have concrete, logical explanations so I won't be blamed or found wrong.
- I must worry to be safe.
- Nothing will hurt me if I keep thinking the same thing over and over.
- I don't trust my intuition.
- I am disconnected from the source.
- My partner is embarrassed by me.
- If they find out I am intuitive, I will have to run away.
- I must put up a façade so the real me is not seen.
- I must obey.
- I have an obligation to obey.
- I can't say no.
- I must do everything that is asked of me.
- It's not okay to say no.
- I can't ask for help; it will be used against me.
- I must leave if I might be obligated.
- I must stay in the shadows.
- I resent people who make demands of me.
- I resent people who try to obligate me.
- I resent people who try to manipulate me.
- I feel guilty if I don't do what others want.

Chapter 12: Pineal Gland Wellness and Third Eye Activation

According to one of the research papers I read, the scientists concluded that no viable allopathic therapy is available for reversing pineal gland calcification. And there is no current research on therapies for decalcifying the pineal gland. The scientists went on to say that the decalcification of the pineal gland has been relegated to complementary medicine.

Intuition and your health are affected by a calcified pineal gland. If the pineal gland is calcified, the third eye chakra will not be in balance and will not work harmoniously. Fluoride ingestion is a component of pineal gland calcification, and removing fluoride from your body and environment makes sense.[23] Fluoride is in food, pesticides, water, toothpaste, dental work, clothing, makeup, cooking utensils, medicines, etc.

---

[23] Tan, D. X., Xu, B., Zhou, X., & Reiter, R. J. (2018). Pineal Calcification, Melatonin Production, Aging, Associated Health Consequences and Rejuvenation of the Pineal Gland. *Molecules (Basel, Switzerland), 23(2), 301.* Available from https://doi.org/10.3390/molecules23020301

Supporting Pineal Gland Wellness

I am a spiritual author, teacher and healer, not a medical doctor or nutritionist. The list below relies upon available nutritional information, my spiritual work, scientific research and common sense. Common sense tells me that removing fluoride from your body and life is a good first step for pineal gland wellness. I use a water filter at home that removes 85-97% of the fluoride from my water.

- I request fluoride-free dentistry.
- I eat organic whole foods when available (pesticides have fluoride).
- I lower my stress using Remen Q̄, exercise, meditation and breathing techniques (stress causes an abnormal release of melatonin).[24]
- I use an essential oil blend called Third Eye Activation Balm* that facilitates the pineal gland function before bed. The blend appears to help with my sleep.
  *The balm is available for purchase at www.peacealchemist.com/store.
- I use fluoride-free toothpaste (I have to order it online; it is no longer readily available in the drug, grocery and natural food stores.)
- I take vitamin A and vitamin K2+D3 supplements.[25,26,27]
- I primarily use ceramic, clay, stainless steel, glass and cast-iron cooking utensils. Additionally, I use **unbleached** parchment paper to line

---

[24] Dagnino-Subiabre, A., Orellana, J. A., Carmona-Fontaine, C., Montiel, J., Díaz-Velíz, G., Serón-Ferré, M., Wyneken, U., Concha, M. L., & Aboitiz, F. (2006). Chronic Stress Decreases the Expression of Sympathetic Markers in the Pineal Gland and Increases Plasma Melatonin Concentration in Rats. *Journal of neurochemistry, 97(5), 1279–1287*.
Available from https://doi.org/10.1111/j.1471-4159.2006.03787.x

[25] Higdon, J (2000). Vitamin K. Linus Pauling Institute Oregon State University. Available from https://lpi.oregonstate.edu/mic/vitamins/vitamin-K#skeletal-formation-soft-tissue-calcification-prevention

[26] Huiberts, L, Smolders, K (2021). Effects of Vitamin D on Mood and Sleep in the Healthy Population: Interpretations from the Serotonergic Pathway. *Sleep Medicine Reviews, Volume 55,101379*, ISSN 1087-0792. Available from https://doi.org/10.1016/j.smrv.2020.101379

[27] Guo, X., Wang, H., Xu, J., & Hua, H. (2022). Impacts of Vitamin A Deficiency on Biological Rhythms: Insights from the Literature. *Frontiers in nutrition, 9, 886244*. Available from https://doi.org/10.3389/fnut.2022.886244

baking pans. Bleached parchment has PFAs (Per**fluoro**octanoic Acid) used in its processing.
- I use energy techniques to facilitate the energetic functioning of the pineal gland chakra. I practice Reiki, Pranic Healing, and an activation technique I learned during my Inner Peace Journey.
- I stop using electronic devices (cell phone, laptop, eReader, etc.) one hour before bed.
- Daily, I take a teaspoon of **organic** tamarind paste in warm water. Tamarind enhances the urinary excretion of fluoride.[28]
- I am on a journey to inner peace, and as such, I am a work in process. I work to transmute fears, emotional states, and limiting patterns frequently. I am developing patience with myself.
- If I have to buy bottled water while traveling, I look for water that has undergone reverse osmosis. Reverse osmosis removes 85-92% of fluoride in the water.
- I use 1 mg of time-release melatonin.

All of the above practices are variable. I follow my inner guidance as to when to stop for a while and when to pick up the use again.

---

[28] Khandare, A. L., Rao, G. S., & Lakshmaiah, N. (2002). Effect of Tamarind Ingestion on Fluoride Excretion in Humans. *European Journal of Clinical Nutrition*, 56(1), 82–85. Available from https://doi.org/10.1038/sj.ejcn.1601287

How Do You Know if Your Third Eye is Opening and Activated?

As you go through the exercises to transform limiting patterns and adjust to the physical world around you to support a healthy pineal gland, the third eye will begin the process of opening and activating. This opening will begin to bring in new experiences.

When your third eye activates, you may experience some or all of the following:

- Occasional painless pressure in the center of your forehead
- See colors and energy waves around all things from nature
- See air prana – this will look like either brilliant sparkles or tiny brilliant tadpoles in the air.
- A flow of creative ideas
- Visualize – your ability to visualize takes on a new level of clarity
- Vivid dreams
- Synchronistic events may happen frequently; for example, you think of someone, and they call. A common thing that happens to me is that I will do an emotional patterns writeup, and the next day, someone appears in my life needing that information.
- Your senses may become enhanced; for example, you become sensitive to light and smell. Taste and hearing are enhanced.
- A feeling that you need to spend time alone or in nature to recharge.
- Connecting a future outcome to current actions or patterns.
- Accelerated spiritual growth
- A profound feeling of compassion toward others.
- An increased interest in understanding our universe
- As you progress on your Inner Peace Journey, you will acquire one and maybe experience all the clairs. A clair(s) will become part of the flow of your daily life. You may begin to experience multiple clairs and the progression of a clair's development. For example, early in life, I could smell a disease. Later in life, I began to smell higher vibrational energies. I would enter the doorway of my home, and the smell of roses would be very prevalent (There were no roses near my home in the winter in the Pacific Northwest.).

I advocate for an organic approach to opening and activating your third eye. This approach will facilitate changes throughout your energy system, not just one chakra center. This approach maintains harmony and balance. The third eye will activate and open as you transmute limiting patterns, support your pineal gland wellness, and develop a consistent spiritual practice (meditation, Inner Peace Journey Work, yoga, Reiki, breathwork, etc.).

Glossary

Aura – An aura is a field of energy that surrounds and interpenetrates the physical body of living things. Some traditions believe the aura reflects an emotional, physical, mental or spiritual state as a luminous emanation that can be perceived as a colored halo. The colors seen in the halo or field represent certain qualities. For example, a red light seen around the heart could mean anger is being held in the heart.

Beingness – Beingness is the flow of creative principles, manifesting as an awareness of self beyond identity. Our essence expresses the creative principle of memory and our choice in each moment.

Bypass – A bypass is a state where you believe you have released or cleared a state of non-peace and later discover that the change was temporary[29]. For example, you believe 'I am not good enough.' Perhaps you have used an emotional release technique to replace that created pattern with 'I'm good enough.' You believe that the created pattern has cleared, and then you discover that it returns the next time a trigger for 'not being good enough' is encountered. You may feel let down, disappointed, angry, betrayed, and untrusting if you have experienced a bypass. A bypass does not get to the underlying trauma that created the limiting pattern. A bypass does not get to the multiple traumas that are part of your experience of a limiting pattern.

A bypass may cause a person to be deceived into thinking that they can stop ongoing medical care. A bypass may mask symptoms of a serious chronic disease, thus causing a delay in treatment.

How do you know if you have set up a bypass? After transmuting a limiting pattern, lean-in or recall another example of the limiting pattern you are working on. When you lean-in, what do you feel in your body (see page 130)? What do you "see/feel/hear" in your inner vision/knowing? If you can still clearly visualize or feel the original limiting pattern, you have not completed the process. You will need to do more Remen $\bar{Q}$.

---

[29] Moore, Valeria (2021). *The Remen $\bar{Q}$ Method: An Easy Do It Yourself Process to Create Inner Peace and Change Your Reality*. Keizer, Oregon, USA; Three Moons Publishing

After you have transmuted the limiting pattern to peace and leaned-into the limiting pattern, recheck the limiting pattern after a sleep cycle to see if you have set up a bypass. The memory should have faded into a ghost-like shadow or a vague impression. Sometimes, you may have lost the memory of it altogether.

Chakra – There are many chakras in our subtle energy body (there are several schools of thought on how many). Chakras are energy centers in your body that correspond to bundles of nerves, major organs, endocrine glands and areas of our energetic body. The chakra receives, transmutes, and distributes prana, life force energy that energizes the physical body. The chakra receives a convergence of life force energy that flows through the nadis. The functioning of the chakras and nadis (energy channels that carry life force energy throughout the subtle body) is affected by the physical, mental and emotional bodies. The classical chakras (root, sacral, solar plexus, heart, throat, third eye, and crown) are associated with specific emotions that derive from the physical function associated with the chakra.

Creative Core - We are born with the ability to create and freely access inner wisdom, our creative core. Our creative core is the flow of inspiration and creativity from all of our bodies. We are born with transparent processes that allow us creativity and intuition based on physical, emotional, mental, and subtle body development.

Created Patterns (Beliefs) - A created pattern is a conceptual identification statement that underlies a behavior done over and over again. For example, a created pattern may be the ritual of drinking coffee first thing in the morning. The created pattern identifies as 'I must have my coffee first thing in the morning.' A created pattern may be feeling betrayed by "friends" repeatedly. The created pattern would then identify as 'My friends betray me.' This created pattern repeatedly tells a story of hurt and harm to prove a victim's status. The ritual of drinking a cup of coffee in the morning may not be limiting. However, the feeling and the created pattern of being betrayed by friends may have locked this person into a cycle of victim identity. This created pattern may be limiting.

The term "created patterns" reflects a shift from using the word '**beliefs**.' Words carry energy, and one of the aspects of the word 'belief(s)' is that it does not globally imply ownership. All 'beliefs' are patterns of creation by the individual holding them regardless of the origin. Ownership, awareness of how their heart feels and the willingness to change a created pattern are essential if a person is genuinely committed to transmuting their state of non-peace.

The foundation of all limiting created patterns is fear(s). To stay safe, you adapt your life and responses to those patterns and create emotional states and multiple created patterns. The origin of fears, created patterns, and emotional states is not always from your life experiences. These limiting patterns may be passed down to you from your ancestry through either conception trauma, ancestral life experience or epigenetics.

Emotional Pathophysiology – Emotional pathophysiology looks at the physiological functions of an anatomical structure, for instance, the pineal gland, heart, spleen, etc., and what is emotionally held there at the functional level. Emotional pathophysiology is a deeper evaluation and gets to the root of the emotional patterns of disease. The impaired state of the pineal gland functions evaluated in this book is pre-disease.

Emotional Release Therapy – Emotional release therapy is the generic term used to describe energetic processes that use a specific method of releasing stuck emotions or trauma that create dysfunction — examples: Reference Point Therapy, Emotional Freedom Technique, etc.

Emotional States – Emotional States is the term I use in my book <u>Emotional Patterns</u>[30] to describe a set of vignettes of emotional wounds or trauma a person has experienced before getting a disease. Each disease can have multiple emotional states, fears, and created patterns.

The nature of all diseases is that we have had an experience and have not understood or learned the higher nature of the event. We have taken in the suffering and created an identity around the trauma. The value of emotional states is that they reference a conceptual grouping of created patterns within a vignette of behavior. Created patterns may be culturally biased in their wording and may not resonate with the person. For example bowing to another person may be a sign of respect and honor in one country, but in another, it is considered an act of subservience. So, a set of beliefs around a physical act may differ across world cultures. The emotional state defines the evolution of fears and beliefs into behaviors that transcend the

---

[30] Moore, Valeria (2021). *Emotional Patterns: Fears, Emotional States and Created Patterns (Beliefs) by Disease, Disorder and Trauma Formerly Healer Wisdom Revision 1*. Keizer, Oregon, USA; Three Moons Publishing.

culture. Emotional states allow for translation into the respective value system. A person may resonate with all the emotional states, none, or an aspect.

Emotional States may have a masculine or feminine nature. The masculine or feminine nature does not mean a woman can have only the feminine or a man only the masculine. It means a person's feminine or masculine aspect reflects that emotional state. A person may be out of balance concerning the masculine or feminine aspects of self. For example, if the masculine is weak, they have many doubts. They doubt their abilities and capability to do things. There is a feeling of being intimidated by life, and moving forward is difficult. They fear putting themselves out there because they 'know' they will fail, so they don't even try to accomplish things. With a weak masculine side, one must show off attributes and accomplishments. People with a weak feminine put a low value on others, and they do not give. There is a predisposition to be selfish, greedy, and closed off from people. Also, the weak feminine does not take responsibility for their actions but blames others for their problems.

An emotional state may hold many beliefs. Beliefs come together synergistically and create an amplified experience within the body. For example, a person has the created pattern 'I hate Aunt Edith.' Along with that belief, there is a reason for the hatred. Maybe the belief is based on the fact that Aunt Edith betrayed them. So, they believe 'Aunt Edith betrayed me.' Depending on the nature of the betrayal, the person may also believe that 'Women betray me.' All of the beliefs have a different vibrational quality that synergistically amplifies the energy of an emotional state. A single belief is limiting but may not produce a powerful shift. When different beliefs combine, the energy is amplified and the result may be disease.

The goal of the Emotional State information is to help you recognize a pattern(s) before the disease happens. Awareness of that pattern opens the door to begin a process of transmutation.

Emotional Wounding (may also be called 'wounding') – Emotional wounding results from a traumatizing or harmful experience (or set of experiences) that causes mental and psychological pain. Various traumatic, personal struggles or distressing experiences may cause these wounds. Trauma may include abuse (physical, emotional, or sexual), neglect, loss of a loved one, accidents, witnessing violence, or any event that feels overwhelming and unsafe. Personal struggles may include chronic illness, financial difficulties, discrimination, and more. Distressing experiences may include betrayal, grief, rejection, bullying, or hurtful relationship experiences such as living with a narcissist. The wound experienced over time or with significant intensity may cause different physical and energetic bodies to create a vibrational frequency representing a limiting pattern to become anchored in your body. The emotional wound will always affect the heart and different aspects of the body that resonate with the wound's vibration.

Epigenetics – Epigenetics is the study of inherited changes that are not changes to the genes. Instead, the inherited change affects how the gene is expressed. The change in expression is due to a chemical attached to the DNA. This chemical change, epigenetic tag, may be inherited. For example, a person's ancestors may have experienced a severe famine and survived a bitter winter with very little food. The stress would have created epigenetic tags. Epigenetic tags are added to genes and affect how those genes are expressed. The grandchildren born to these ancestors will inherit the epigenetic tags that developed due to insufficient food and the fear of starvation. The grandchildren may live with the need to put away more food than is necessary. They may also experience anxiety around food.

Fears - At the core of every emotional state or created pattern (belief) is a historical trauma(s) or wounding. Historical trauma or wounding may come from your ancestry or a recent life experience. You frame your human experience of trauma within your familial, cultural, geopolitical, dogmatic or institutional rules. You may experience an instinctual response or fear if the trauma is physically threatening. That fear is then held in your mental, emotional and physical bodies. For example, you may have experienced severe food deprivation during a war. You may have experienced the fear of dying from starvation for a prolonged period.

After the war passed and food became readily available, you may continue experiencing the fear of dying from starvation. You may hoard food. You may feel like you never have enough food in your cabinets. You chastise those around you for wasting food. You may eat food your body does not need because you cannot bear seeing it go to waste. You may experience anxiety around events where food is abundant. Some of the fears being experienced are fear of dying, fear of being alone, fear of starving, fear of not having enough, fear of having food taken away, and more. These fears will play out in the different bodies. You may think (mental body) frequently about food: getting food, storing food, preparing food, eating, etc. You may feel anxious and worry (emotional body) about food. The anxiety and worry over time will crystallize into digestion and pancreatic issues (physical body).

Field – A field is a subtly defined multi-dimensional space of influence. If I say, 'I am witness to the field of intention,' I have made an intention with an area of influence. A relationship between two people would also be a field. The relationship occupies space and contains energy, creating an area of influence, a field.

Harmony – In a state of harmony, you experience the flow of the creative principle; you experience grace. When you flow with the river of life, the creative principle, you experience the knowing of our nature. Our essence expresses the creative principles of memory and our choices in each moment.

Heart-Soul Wisdom – This is the energetic bridge or portal between your intuitive heart and the Universal Wisdom/time continuum. This portal may be requested and activated for use. Universal Wisdom, when requested, will flow across this portal and into your awareness when you have reached the intersection of the Dancing with the Ego and the Self-Realization stage of intuition development.

Inner Peace Journey – The Inner Peace Journey is a lifelong process of seeking and cultivating inner calm and joy. Inner peace isn't a destination you reach, and you are done. It starts with a call from the heart. The heart feels a deep need to experience the infinite expansion of meditation, a spiritual practice, a connection to our divinity, to develop and know the wisdom of the ancients, to release the emotional energies that bind our hearts, and more. This journey may involve practices listed in the definition of Inner Peace Journey Work below and more. These practices facilitate the development of self-awareness, harmony, balance, and connecting with a sense of purpose.

Inner Peace Journey Work – Inner Peace Journey Work is a discovery process of understanding and knowing self. The wisdom of self leads to an understanding of the limiting patterns we hold: fears, limiting beliefs or patterns, traumas, thoughts, and potential motivations. That understanding is then used to transmute our emotional wounds using meditation, breathwork, journaling, bodywork, a spiritual practice, yoga, qigong, being in nature, art therapy, non-dualistic emotional transmutation work (Remen $\bar{Q}$), etc. Inner Peace Journey Work brings you inner peace, greater creativity, increased self-awareness, improved relationships, and more.

Magical Thinking -- Relegates life's destiny to invisible superstitious forces for which you have no responsibility. Magical thinking may be how you coped with childhood trauma. The following are examples of magical thinking:

- When I win the lottery, all my problems will go away.
- If I lose five more pounds, my partner will love me.
- If I do what my husband tells me, he won't hit me again.
- If I am a better person, my partner won't get drunk.
- If I hear an owl hoot three times, I will die.
- If I ignore this problem, it will all go away.
- If I ignore this pain, it will go away.
- When I carry my crystal, no one will hurt me.
- My birth parents will show up someday and take me home.
- I must have my special necklace to stop bad things from happening.

Modality – A modality is a particular way that something is done. The use of 'modality' in this book refers to alternative or complementary healing methods. Reiki, Pranic Healing, Healing Touch Therapy, Emotional Freedom Technique, Remen $\bar{Q}$, etc., are examples of modalities.

Nadis – These are subtle energy body channels, in conjunction with the chakras, carry life force or prana throughout the body.

Past Life Regression – A past life regression uses hypnosis to access memories of a past life. Past life regressions may be used to access a past life that may be the source of trauma in the current life.

Relationship – A relationship is a continuum of experience in space and time. A relationship is not a static feedback loop. Instead, a relationship is an energy flow between connecting entities that continually creates your reality. You have many relationships. You have a relationship with people and things you know and don't know. For example, you have a relationship with a store clerk you see on Wednesday while grocery shopping. You may not know her name, but you have a relationship. Everyone who has touched your life has a relationship with you. You may not know the leadership of your country, but you have a relationship with them because they, directly and indirectly, influence your life. A relationship can also be non-human.

When someone close to you dies, and you grieve their passing, you are grieving the change in the relationship.

Spiritual Bypass – A spiritual bypass is a defense mechanism that facilitates hiding behind a spiritual practice to avoid doing Inner Peace Journey Work. This practice has the effect of stopping your spiritual and inner growth. Below are some aspects of a spiritual bypass:

- Diverts and stops you from your inner work.
- You take shortcuts with your inner work and avoid dealing with difficult feelings. Doesn't engage in transmuting difficult emotions.
- Uses the phrase "you just need to let go" to dismiss the suffering of others.
- Uses metaphysical modality creations as a defense mechanism to divert from doing the hard inner work.
- Abrogates their ownership, decision making and responsibility to a metaphysical practice.
- Uses spiritual experiences to avoid integration of spiritual wisdom.

Time Continuum – The time continuum is also known as the **Akashic Record, Universal Wisdom or Zero Point Energy field**. This field holds the vibrational frequencies of all that has or will happen in the All.

Transmutation – The definition from Merriam-Webster dictionary is to change or alter in form, appearance, or nature, especially to a higher form. In this book, Remen $\overline{Q}$ is used as a tool of transmutation. Remen $\overline{Q}$ moves you from non-peace to peace, a higher form of being, an elevated vibration. This elevated vibration is your natural state.

Trauma Response – A trauma response is the way we cope with traumatic experiences. [31]

Trigger – A trigger is a connection or link to trauma from your current life or ancestry that provokes an emotional response. A trigger can be a physical item, a sound, a word, a smell, an image, a color, a person's voice, etc. For example, standing in line at a store, the woman in front of you is wear-

---

[31] Trauma - Reaction and recovery. (n.d.). Better Health Channel. Retrieved March 15, 2024, from
https://www.betterhealth.vic.gov.au/health/conditionsandtreatments/trauma-reaction-and-recovery

ing perfume that reminds you of an aunt you loved. You are immediately overwhelmed with grief. That aunt passed away many years ago, and you immediately feel overwhelming sadness. The smell of the perfume was a trigger for your stuck grief.

Universal Wisdom – The Universal Wisdom is also known as the **Akashic Record, Time Continuum or Zero Point Energy field**. This field holds the vibrational frequencies of all that has or will happen in the All.

Wounded Creative Core - The wounding of our creative core is the adaptation we made to survive institutional abuse. Institutions (schools, governments, familial, cultures and religious dogma) constrain the creative core and destroy inspiration, creativity and joy through shame, humiliation, rejection, shunning, violence and more. When a child experiences these controlling institutional tools, the creative core is wounded, and the creative flow is severely impaired. I have named this trauma the Wounded Creative Core. The Wounded Creative Core is a meta-state in many diseases.

Resources

Body Scans

A body scan is done by entering a light meditational state and moving your awareness to the top of your head. You can use the 'breathe into presence' technique described in the Remen $\bar{Q}$ process.[32] You then move your awareness slowly through your body and notice what feels different, resistant, or uncomfortable. You may get impressions that are emotional, energetic, or physical.

You can use body scanning as another tool for achieving wellness. Once you have done the initial scan, you can go back to the areas with qualities that did not flow. Focusing your awareness into a place of resistance, ask the question in your inner voice, "What is emotionally held here?" Use your journal to make a note of the information you gather. Then, use that information as a point of non-peace and Remen $\bar{Q}$ the non-peace until there is flow in that part of the body. This process may take some practice.

The body scan is a meditative process and can be used to transmute tension with each area of awareness in your body.

---

[32] Moore, Valeria (2021). *The Remen $\bar{Q}$ Method: An Easy Do-It-Yourself Process to Create Inner Peace and Change Your Reality*. Keizer, Oregon, USA; Three Moons Publishing.

Emotional Patterns

<u>Emotional Patterns: Fears, Emotional States and Created Patterns (Beliefs) by Disease, Disorder and Trauma Formerly Healer Wisdom Revision 1</u> is the aggregation of fears, created patterns(beliefs) and emotional states of diseases and disorders. The book is available from your independent bookstore or Amazon. The book holds 500 different write-ups. The online database currently has over 1000 write-ups and is growing. The online book also allows searching for related disorders and symptoms or exploring system-level categories, such as searching for all disorders in the digestive system. Please see the information on this website to access the website database.

Many of us live our lives unconsciously and ignore the messages our body is sending us. We take the pain pill or antacid and go about our lives. Even after developing a disease, we ignore the information our body sends. If the heart pain becomes too much, we numb the heart's messages of emotional wounding. The emotional patterns' material aims to provide a possible recognition of patterns in a person's life that will trigger an awareness of the wound being held. That awareness, if the person chooses, provides the point of non-peace that can then be transmuted to peace using Remen $\overline{Q}$.

https://emotionalpatterns.com

Grounding Meditation

Start by sitting comfortably upright in a chair (If you cannot sit at the moment, this can also be done standing.). Take several slow, deep belly breaths. Ease yourself into doing belly breathing as your normal breath. Now, imagine a beam of light entering your crown. The beam of light moves through your body and out the bottoms of your feet. The beam of light moves through the floor and into the earth. The beam of light travels to the center of the earth. Become aware of the earth's nurturance. Now imagine the energy of being ungrounded (overwhelmed, anxious, disconnected, etc.) traveling down the beam of light and into the earth. Imagine giving those energies to the earth for transmutation. Now, bring back the beam of light up through your feet. Watch as the beam of light moves up your legs and into the lower part of your body, bringing safety and security. The light beam continues traveling up your body and out the top of your head where it entered. Now, open your eyes slowly and stretch your arms and legs.

Journaling

*The information in this chapter comes from my forthcoming book <u>Creating a Foundation for Inner Peace</u>.

Journaling is a way to self-awareness. *Self-awareness is an opening to an understanding of our nature by being the observer and witness to our lives. The process of self-awareness asks that we not judge ourselves or engage in self-criticism.*

When you journal, you listen to your heart's transmission of wisdom beyond your logical thinking processes. *Putting your pen on the journal page opens a sacred connection that joins the heart with the higher self's wisdom if that is your intention. This physical, mental, and spiritual connection allows accessing wisdom beyond the boundaries of the logical mind to reveal a knowing beyond the logical mind. This type of information is beyond fear. You can ask for guidance from the aspect of self that you encounter beyond these boundaries. When you do this, write the question and then write down what comes to mind as you open to reflecting on the answer.*

Journaling allows you to focus your thoughts and yields insights into the limiting patterns you may be holding. *When journaling, you may record feelings and behaviors that limit you. Your awareness of what you hold develops as you write about those limiting patterns. Once you have the awareness of limiting patterns, you have a choice. You may choose to transmute those limiting patterns or not. Choosing not to transmute limiting patterns is a determination that you will experience those patterns again.*

Journaling also allows you to do the following:

- See your Inner Peace Journey progress
- Explore your identity, feelings, motivations, values, and relationship interactions.

- Access the subconscious
- Ask questions that you need to ask and then record the answers
- Explore your feelings without judgment
- Transmute your limiting patterns as you write; this is a gift from the journaling process. As you write, you are listening with your heart and that listening can create a transmutation.*

See Glossary page 122 for more information

You limit your life when you say you can't journal, and journaling would benefit your inner work. You are putting a boundary around what you are allowing yourself to experience. You are letting fear control your life and stopping the flow of life force.

When you sit to journal, your inner voice may say, 'I can't do journaling,' 'this is a waste of time,' 'I have nothing to say,' etc. This voice is the inner critic stopping you from listening to your heart-soul wisdom.* The inner critic may become quite vocal while you are learning to journal. If you are getting frustrated or hearing non-peace from your inner voice, write that down and use the Remen $\overline{Q}$ process to transmute to neutral or peace. Write down what your inner critic is telling you. Then Remen $\overline{Q}$, the non-peace you have just experienced. After you feel peace, lean-in to the prior statements made by your inner critic and see if the inner critic is now silent or has more to say

. *See Glossary page 120 for more information*

Daily Practice

Sitting with your journal daily, even for a few minutes, is good practice. Write down anything encountered from the day or the previous day that created non-peace and Remen $\overline{Q}$ any heart contractions. Record the results. If the non-peace you are transmuting has been an ongoing pattern, you may want to go back and check that pattern a few days later and see if any non-peace is left.

Use the daily check-in to create a space for all the thoughts running around in your head. It's OK that they may not make any sense. If the thoughts are judgmental and demanding, use Remen $\overline{Q}$ to transmute them to peace.

Now, check in with your heart. After you have done the daily check-in, is there something bothering you? For example, is there something that caused you to feel guilty, anxious, etc.? This state of awareness is what I call journal meditation. If states of non-peace arise, Remen $\bar{Q}$ the non-peace and, if need be, lean-in.

This brief exploration of journaling is not intended to be a definitive essay. Therefore, I urge you to read <u>The Artist Way: A Spiritual Path to Higher Creativity</u> by Julia Cameron.[33] For me, journaling is about gaining insight into the journey to peace. Ms. Cameron's book explores journaling as a tool for unblocking your creativity. I experience my most profound sense of peace when I am creating. The journey to peace may well be a journey to creativity.

---

[33] Cameron, J. (2020a). *The Artist's Way: A Spiritual Path to Higher Creativity.* Souvenir Press.

Leaning-In

Per the website PlainEnglish.com, "lean-into" is defined as an expression that means to embrace, to fully engage with, or to actively pursue something, like an idea, a concept, a situation, a course of action. "Lean-into" implies a proactive and enthusiastic approach to something rather than a passive, cautious, or hesitant approach.[34]

When you "lean-in" in Remen $\overline{Q}$, you proactively work to transmute any potential bypasses. One of the unfortunate aspects of emotional release therapies, and some physical healing modalities as well, is that many of them create a bypass. This bypass means that you still have the pattern of non-peace; a feeling of calm or love now hides it, which may be backed up by a physical form of validation, such as muscle testing. Additional work may be needed to transmute long-standing limiting patterns.

You do this additional work by recalling an experience of the limiting pattern that you just transmuted to peace. What do you feel in your body? What do you "see/feel/hear" in your inner knowing? If you feel a contraction in your heart or elsewhere, you have set up a bypass. If you can clearly "see/feel/hear" the experience, you have set up a bypass. If you can still visualize, feel or hear the original limitation you transmuted, you have not completed the process of transmuting the non-peace pattern.

If the limiting pattern you are working to transmute has been with you for a long time, you have experienced it many times. Each time you experience the limiting pattern, it is a different vibrational frequency. If the vibrational frequency is different, then you will need to lean-in. For example, the vibrational frequency of all the limiting patterns you hold of "not good enough" may be similar enough that they will transmute with Remen $\overline{Q}$ after a few rounds. Conversely, they may not be and will require leaning-in.

After you have transmuted the limiting pattern to peace, recheck the limiting pattern by feeling it in your heart. The memory should have faded into a ghost-like shadow or a vague impression. Sometimes, you may have lost

---

[34] Lean-in. (2023, November 9). Plain English. https://plainenglish.com/expressions/lean-into/

the memory of it altogether. If not, you need to do additional rounds of Remen $\bar{Q}$. Then, repeat the check-in process. If you feel peace, neutral or calm, you may be complete. I suggest you review that limiting pattern again after a sleep cycle or a few days later.

About the Author

Valeria Moore is a consciousness researcher, author, teacher, healing arts practitioner, developer of Remen Q̄, peace alchemist and journeyer. Valeria has explored the foundations of our consciousness since the 1970s and shared her explorations with people worldwide. Valeria has never used just one path to discover the wisdom of the ancients. Instead, she believes many traditions hold foundational wisdom that moves us towards understanding our nature. Valeria trained in many healing modalities. Each one of these healing methods added to her understanding of our nature.

Valeria has been a practitioner and teacher of metaphysical healing modalities, meditation and emotional release techniques for 50+ years. She started exploring the emotional foundations of disease in the early 2000s. She has written over 1,000 emotional pattern write-ups, which include fears, emotional states, and created patterns (beliefs). In 2013, she began a six-year journey to develop a transmutation modality. That modality, Remen Q̄, is based on an intention of peace.

Valeria holds a degree in computer and information sciences from the University of California.

Valeria retired in 2017 and immediately started writing. She plans many personal transformation books in the coming years. She recently published The Remen Q̄ Method: An Easy Do-It-Yourself Process to Create Inner Peace and Change Your Reality. Healer Wisdom, first published in 2005, became Emotional Patterns: Fears, Emotional States and Created Patterns (Beliefs) by Disease, Disorder and Trauma, published in 2019. Billy Visits the Farmer's Market: Adventures of Billy, Lilly, Milly and Mr. Ely. The children's book offers a brief science of an aspect of our environment at the end of the book. You can check https://peacealchemist.com to see what books are in the works and their expected publishing dates, which are always too optimistic.

Valeria lives in Oregon with her life partner. She has two daughters and five fantastic grandchildren. She enjoys kayaking, hiking, painting, sewing, gardening and playing with her grandchildren.

Contacting Valeria and Additional Support

If you have questions about this book, Remen Q̄ or <u>Emotional Patterns,</u> email mail@peacealchemist.com.

For ongoing articles, classes, new podcasts, and book updates, go to https://peacealchemist.com.

If you have a question about material in this book, email me at mail@peacealchemist.com. The question may go into a FAQ page unless you tell me it is confidential. I will not use a name if I use a question on the FAQ page.

You can request a class or one-on-one support from one of the Remen Q̄ teachers using the contact information on the teacher's page:

https://peacealchemist.com/remen-q%cc%85-teachers/ .

If this book has moved you forward on your Inner Peace Journey, please leave a review on Amazon.

By joining my mail list you get notification of new articles, new books, new classes, etc. You can sign up on my website https://peacealchemist.com.

Appendices

Appendix A: About the Pineal Gland

What and Where is the Pineal Gland?

The pineal gland is a pea-sized endocrine gland located in the brain's center. It secretes hormones into the bloodstream. Hormones are messengers of control and regulation. Hormones tell your body what to do and when to do it. The primary hormone emitted by the pineal gland is melatonin, now considered the master hormone by some researchers.[35]

The pineal gland is located outside of the blood-brain barrier. The pineal gland is only second to the kidneys in the volume of blood flow going through it. Being outside the blood-brain barrier exposes the pineal gland to toxins that may have entered the blood.

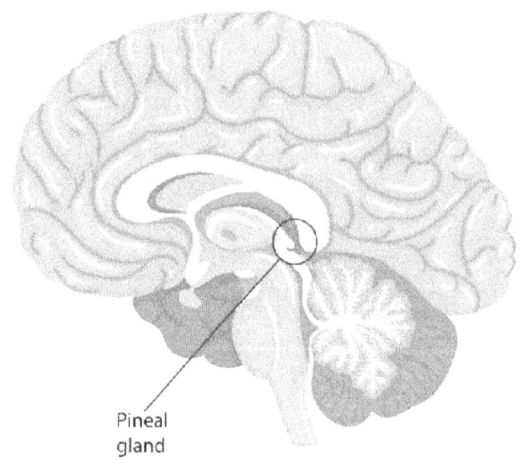

---

[35] Arendt J, Aulinas A. *Physiology of the Pineal Gland and Melatonin*. [Updated 2022 Oct 30]. In: Feingold KR, Anawalt B, Blackman MR, et al., editors. Endotext [Internet]. South Dartmouth (MA): MDText.com, Inc.; 2000-. Available from: https://www.ncbi.nlm.nih.gov/books/NBK550972/

What Does the Pineal Gland Do?

The primary function of the pineal gland is to receive and convey information about the current light-dark cycle from the environment via the production and secretion of melatonin cyclically at night (circadian rhythm). Melatonin rises in the evening and continues rising for the next several hours. Light hitting the retina signals the pineal gland to stop producing melatonin. This regulation of melatonin is why we feel more awake during the day and sleepy at night.[36]

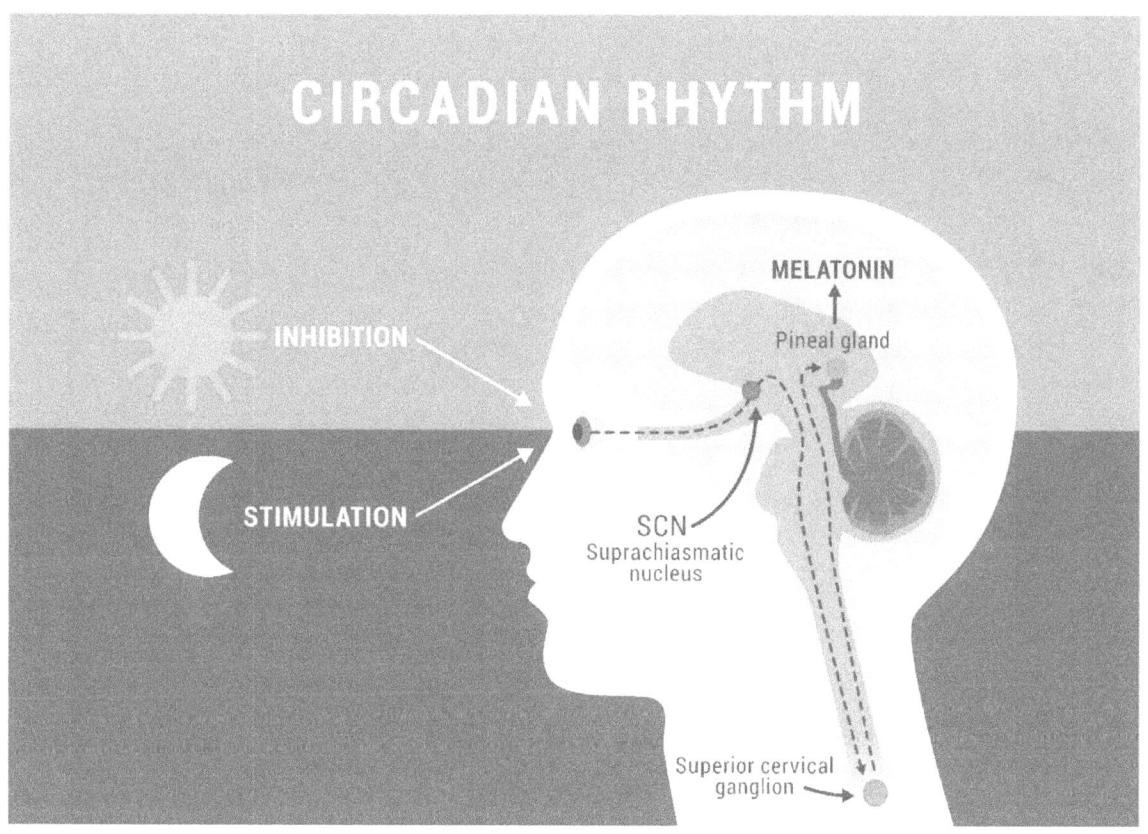

---

[36] Arendt J, Aulinas A.(2022). *Physiology of the Pineal Gland and Melatonin.* Feingold KR, Anawalt B, Blackman MR, et al., editors. Endotext [Internet]. South Dartmouth (MA): MDText.com, Inc.; 2000. Available from https://www.ncbi.nlm.nih.gov/books/NBK550972/

Melatonin has several other functions addressed in Appendix D. Appendix D also explores the emotional pathophysiology of the function when it becomes dysregulated.

Working with Emotional Patterns and Emotional Pathophysiology

The following chapters present fears, emotional states and created patterns that have potentially affected the pineal gland. To work with this material, set aside some quiet time; a half hour to an hour should be adequate for a session and have a journal handy. Read the Repeating Patterns* and Emotional Patterns (Emotional States, Fears, and Created Patterns) sequentially. After reading a statement, stop for a moment and feel your heart and body. Is there a new contraction or non-peace feeling? If so, Remen Q̄ the non-peace until you are calm, neutral or at peace. See Chapter 5, page 25, for Remen Q̄ instructions.

Repeating patterns are life trends a person may experience if they have a specific disease or disorder.

Appendix B: Physical Diseases, Disorders and the Associated Emotional Patterns of the Pineal Gland

Pineal gland calcification causes a lowering of melatonin production. The reduction of melatonin production has been found to contribute to the development of the diseases explored in this chapter. This chapter explores the emotional patterns of diseases where research has implicated lower melatonin levels as having a direct link to the development of a disease.[37]

Repeating Patterns

A person with a calcified pineal gland doesn't flow with life and tends to block or put up barriers to the flow. They don't think they can create, so they avoid creating; everything is by the book. They rely on others or institutions for their inner truth. They do not look inward. Their inner voice is shut out and down—Wounded Creative Core. They block receiving or want more than they should. They have faulty filtering and a lack of discernment. They either lack control or tend to over-control. They have a sense of time that is dysregulated. For example they consistently show up for appointments late or very early.

---

[37] Tan, D. X., Xu, B., Zhou, X., & Reiter, R. J. (2018). Pineal Calcification, Melatonin Production, Aging, Associated Health Consequences and Rejuvenation of the Pineal Gland. *Molecules* (Basel, Switzerland), 23(2), 301. Available from https://doi.org/10.3390/molecules23020301

Advanced Sleep Phase Disorder (ASPD)

Advanced Sleep Phase Disorder is a sleep disorder that causes people to go to bed and wake up earlier than most people. People with ASPD have difficulty staying awake in the evening.[38]

Repeating Patterns

Give and receive out of balance, looking for others to fill the hole and make them whole, on guard.

Emotional States

- ❖ Time becomes their enemy. They are always running. Always trying to stay in sync with the world and meet expectations, but they can't. Too many things to do. Too many places to go. If they keep running, they will not have to stop and consider their being. They fear the hurt of considering a life where they missed so much.

- ❖ Hopeless that things will not change or get better. They have given in and given up. They have thrown up blocks to life. Mean people emotionally pummeled them and won't let them out of a prison of guilt and anger.

---

[38] Auger, R. R., Burgess, H. J., Emens, J. S., Deriy, L. V., Thomas, S. M., & Sharkey, K. M. (2015). Clinical Practice Guideline for the Treatment of Intrinsic Circadian Rhythm Sleep-Wake Disorders: Advanced Sleep-Wake Phase Disorder (ASWPD), Delayed Sleep-Wake Phase Disorder (DSWPD), Non-24-Hour Sleep-Wake Rhythm Disorder (N24SWD), and Irregular Sleep-Wake Rhythm Disorder (ISWRD). An Update for 2015: An American Academy of Sleep Medicine Clinical Practice Guideline. *Journal of Clinical Sleep Medicine: JCSM: Official Publication of the American Academy of Sleep Medicine, 11(10), 1199–1236.* Available from https://doi.org/10.5664/jcsm.5100

Fears

- ✦ Fears time
- ✦ Fears of never having enough
- ✦ Fears disappointing others
- ✦ Fears failure
- ✦ Fears self
- ✦ Fears missing out
- ✦ Fears change
- ✦ Fears their pain
- ✦ Fears never being enough
- ✦ Fears life
- ✦ Fears hardship
- ✦ Fears a life sadness
- ✦ Fears being out of control
- ✦ Fears feeling guilty
- ✦ Fears mean people
- ✦ Fears being out of sync

Created Patterns

- I am always missing out.
- I miss opportunities.
- Time is my enemy.
- I never have enough time to do the things I want to do.
- There's never enough time for me.
- There's never enough time.
- People are mean to me.
- My life will never get better.
- I am guilty.
- I am angry at _____.
- I am hopeless.
- I can't fight them anymore.
- I am tired.
- I am trapped.
- If I give in, I can stay in control.
- I let people abuse me.
- I can't let anything new in.

- Everything is out of control.
- I am sad.
- I lead a sad life.
- Life is a struggle.
- I struggle to exist.
- I am a failure.
- If I fail, I will be hurt.
- I must keep busy so as not to look at myself.
- If I have too much time, I will start to think.

Delayed Sleep Phase Disorder(DSPD)

Individuals with delayed sleep phase disorder go to bed and wake up later than most people. DSPD people do not usually fall asleep before 1 or 2 a.m. and wake up late.[39]

Repeating Patterns

Give and receive out of balance, looking for others to fill the hole and make them whole, on guard. (This is the same as advanced sleep phase disorder).

Emotional States

- Just when they thought they were safe, a movement or a sound heightened their awareness. They stay on guard. They don't understand the sounds or the movement. Will it hurt them, or will it go away?

- Hopelessness. Silent voices nag at them — remind them of who they are not. Far away sounds. No structure. No information, no pattern. They feel pulled one way and then another.

- Wanton disregard for others left them with empty space. Worried memories created angst and anxiety. Anger shut them off.

- Short-term meaning to everything. Everything is transitory. They had unreasonable expectations of what others would do for them and

---

[39] Auger, R. R., Burgess, H. J., Emens, J. S., Deriy, L. V., Thomas, S. M., & Sharkey, K. M. (2015). Clinical Practice Guideline for the Treatment of Intrinsic Circadian Rhythm Sleep-Wake Disorders: Advanced Sleep-Wake Phase Disorder (ASWPD), Delayed Sleep-Wake Phase Disorder (DSWPD), Non-24-Hour Sleep-Wake Rhythm Disorder (N24SWD), and Irregular Sleep-Wake Rhythm Disorder (ISWRD). An Update for 2015: An American Academy of Sleep Medicine Clinical Practice Guideline. *Journal of Clinical Sleep Medicine : JCSM: Official Publication of the American Academy of Sleep Medicine*, 11(10), 1199–1236. Available from https://doi.org/10.5664/jcsm.5100

then were never available to return the favor. No balance of in and out flow, give and receive. Expected to only give as a child, received nothing.

Fears

- ✦ Fears anything sudden
- ✦ Fears the unknown
- ✦ Fears the unexplained
- ✦ Fears change
- ✦ Fears of being hurt by sudden movements
- ✦ Fears of not meeting expectations
- ✦ Fears nothingness
- ✦ Fears being caught
- ✦ Fears being trapped
- ✦ Fears being misunderstood
- ✦ Fears of being forced to give
- ✦ Fears of not being good enough
- ✦ Fears of being unloved/unwanted/unneeded
- ✦ Fears depending on anyone or anything
- ✦ Fears inner voice.

Created Patterns

- I am not good enough.
- I must be on guard at all times.
- Sudden sounds mean I will be hurt.
- I am forced against my will to give.
- I never get anything in return for my efforts.
- I am haunted by an inner voice that hates me.
- I am unsupported.
- I must worry to be safe.
- I am unwanted.
- I can't depend on others.
- I am unloved.
- I am forced to give against my will.
- No one respects my needs.

- What I have is not my own; someone always tries to take something from me.
- I am trapped, and I can't escape.
- I am nothing.
- I am invisible.
- I am alone.
- Others use me.
- I am only here so people can use me.
- If I get caught, I will be hurt.
- I never seem to get it right.
- Change is dangerous.
- The unknown is dangerous.
- The unknown always takes from me.
- What I want is sacrificed so others can get what they want.
- I am always last.

Fluoride Toxicity

Fluoride is a component in pineal gland calcification and impairs the pineal gland's functioning.[40]

Repeating Patterns

Impatience, disconnection, ungrounded, selfishness, lack of empathy, does not give, doesn't acknowledge receiving, opinionated.

Emotional States

- ❖ Short temper. Impatience. Irritated with confusing people who do confusing actions. Wants tasks done forthwith, no dilly-dallying or delays. Becomes agitated when delays happen.

- ❖ Hollow words. They have no empathy for others. Becomes irritated when they are expected to give empathy as a condition of socialization.

- ❖ Rough ideas that never really congeal to form a cohesive thought. They are disconnected and ungrounded. Connected means harm, so they float through it all without a heart connection.

- ❖ Hostile judgments that align only with their selfish ideas of receiving or taking – no inclination to give or share. Justified in their holding or keeping.

- ❖ Minimal knowing before they throw in their opinion and declare it the holy truth of all. They will not listen to other opinions and other know-

---

[40] Available from https://doi.org/10.1186/s12940-019-0546-7 Malin, A.J., Bose, S., Busgang, S.A. *et al*. Fluoride Exposure and Sleep Patterns Among Older Adolescents in the United States: a Cross-sectional Study of NHANES 2015–2016. *Environ Health 18, 106* (2019).

ing—tunnel thinking. No other options or information. Leads a restricted life.

- ❖ Hopelessness. Emptiness. Nothing fills them. They get but never receive. Unwanted and unloved.

Fears

- ✦ Fears distraction
- ✦ Fears being found to be lacking
- ✦ Fears confusion
- ✦ Fears failing
- ✦ Fears being overwhelmed
- ✦ Fears being blamed
- ✦ Fears being seen as not worthy
- ✦ Fears taking responsibility for the actions of others
- ✦ Fears vulnerability
- ✦ Fears giving
- ✦ Fears being made to give
- ✦ Fears connection with others
- ✦ Fears change
- ✦ Fears the expectations of love
- ✦ Fears being forced against their will
- ✦ Fears flow
- ✦ Fears others may want from them
- ✦ Fears being obligated
- ✦ Fears of being left behind
- ✦ Fear of losing everything if they receive
- ✦ Fear of being hurt if they receive
- ✦ Fears being alone
- ✦ Fear of connection
- ✦ Fear of being overwhelmed by the needs of another
- ✦ Fears that their truth could be changed
- ✦ Fears being challenged

Created Patterns

- I am unwanted.
- People that challenge me want to humiliate me.

- I am right.
- My truth is infallible.
- Gifts are an obligation.
- Giving is an obligation.
- I resent being obligated.
- I am forced against my will to participate in societal obligations.
- People won't leave me alone; they constantly take my time.
- People try to take from me.
- If I get distracted, I will fail.
- If I get distracted, people will hurt me.
- If I get distracted, people will take from me.
- I'm not good enough.
- I'm not enough.
- Too much and there is nothing but confusion.
- I get confused when I am overwhelmed.
- Confusion keeps me safe.
- If I fail, people will hurt me.
- I get blamed for things I didn't do.
- If I don't do for others, I won't be blamed.
- Obligations are just a way of creating blame.
- I have no control.
- I'm not worthy.
- I'm worthless.
- Other people try to make me responsible for the actions of others.
- Staying away from people is the only way to stay safe.
- If I am weak, people will overrun me.
- If I am seen as weak, people will hurt me.
- If I am seen as weak, people will take from me.
- Giving creates expectations and disappointment.
- Receiving creates expectations and disappointment.
- I am safer alone.
- Love means expectations and disappointment.
- If I let people, they will hurt me.
- I must always be on guard.
- People want to take what I have.
- I am unloved.
- I am unwanted.

- I must judge to be safe.
- Judgment protects me by creating walls that prevent being overrun.
- I can't rest until a job is done.

Hypermelatoninemia

Hypermelatoninemia happens when there is a higher-than-normal peak in nighttime melatonin levels, usually extended into the morning (daylight), compared to normal levels for age and sex.[41]

Repeating Patterns

Alcoholic behavior without the alcohol (starts fights, blames others for their problems, isolation, withdrawal), ACOA, anger, abandoned, loss of connection, emotional blocks to feeling.

Emotional States

- ❖ Falsehoods in life have caused disruptions in their thinking. Feels a sense of animosity toward those who don't care – sees them as weak and amorphous (not standing for the strength of conviction). Heart was falsely led, and they shut down the heart's compassion.

- ❖ Jumped off a cliff too soon — didn't have all the needed facts. They were left lost and confused. They didn't see what they did so wrong. They didn't see the risk. They were criticized and judged as stupid.

- ❖ Just when they thought they had it all together and life figured out, it all came crashing down around their ears. They felt like they lost everything. No one showed up to help, and they were abandoned by friends and family. They never rose to move forward; instead, it became a pity party.

---

[41] Arendt J, Aulinas A. *Physiology of the Pineal Gland and Melatonin*. [Updated 2022 Oct 30]. In: Feingold KR, Anawalt B, Blackman MR, et al., editors. Endotext [Internet]. South Dartmouth (MA): MDText.com, Inc.; 2000-. Available from https://www.ncbi.nlm.nih.gov/books/NBK550972/

- ❖ Wanton disposal (discounting) of the feelings of others. Others reacted with angry words and accusations. They became defensive and hyper-aggressive. Then, they fled from their own aggression and withdrew so they could hide from their own feelings. They are reenacting behavior learned from their alcoholic father. They became afraid of who they had become without the alcohol.

Fears

- ✦ Fears of having their heart hurt
- ✦ Fears being betrayed
- ✦ Fears being lied to
- ✦ Fears being seen as a stooge
- ✦ Fears of being called out for their behavior
- ✦ Fears of being forced into a corner
- ✦ Fears having to confront their feelings
- ✦ Fears themselves
- ✦ Fears becoming like their parent(s)
- ✦ Fears any feelings
- ✦ Fear of failing
- ✦ Fear of becoming what their parent(s) said they would become
- ✦ Fears being alone
- ✦ Fears being abandoned
- ✦ Fears of being accused of being wrong

Created Patterns

- I'm not good enough.
- I'll never be worth anything.
- People rat me out.
- I'm always wrong.
- I always get blamed for bad things that happen.
- I am alone.
- No one understands me.
- People abandon me.
- No one ever shows up for me.
- I'm the victim.
- I'll never amount to a hill of beans.

- I'm trapped.
- I am betrayed.
- People lie to me.
- Compassion is for weak people.
- You've got to take it like a man.
- Big boys/girls don't cry.
- Feelings make you weak.
- You can't let anyone see how you feel.

Hypomelatoninemia

Hypomelatoninemia is a condition in which the body produces abnormally low melatonin levels. Melatonin is released in response to darkness and helps to regulate the sleep-wake cycle. Low melatonin levels can lead to sleep problems, such as insomnia, and other health problems, such as depression, reproduction and anxiety.[42]

Repeating Patterns

Abandoned, betrayed, grief, guilt, unnoticed, doesn't know if they exist.

Emotional States

- ❖ Forgetfulness. Forgot the day. Forgot their life. Forgot so they would not hurt. Forgot so they would not live with the pain and guilt. Isolated with their grief and trauma, they plunged into darkness.

- ❖ Left out, they felt less-than and invisible. They were abandoned by others. They were unaware of why they seemed to be a phantom. Their heart hurt and searched for a connection, but there was no one who wanted that. They were not present. The lack of presence saved them.

- ❖ False impression of connection and caring left them feeling abandoned and betrayed. People lied to them. They were not willing to be there when needed.

Fears

- ✦ Fears remembering
- ✦ Fears knowing
- ✦ Fears their life

---

[42] Arendt J, Aulinas A. *Physiology of the Pineal Gland and Melatonin*. [Updated 2022 Oct 30]. In: Feingold KR, Anawalt B, Blackman MR, et al., editors. Endotext [Internet]. South Dartmouth (MA): MDText.com, Inc.; 2000-. Available from https://www.ncbi.nlm.nih.gov/books/NBK550972/

- ✦ Fears allowing flow
- ✦ Fears the pain of their heart
- ✦ Fears feeling guilty
- ✦ Fears others
- ✦ Fears others reminding them of their pain
- ✦ Fears being invisible
- ✦ Fears being seen
- ✦ Fears being alone
- ✦ Fears being abandoned
- ✦ Fears being present
- ✦ Fears false friends
- ✦ Fears being betrayed
- ✦ Fears no one showing up

Created Patterns

- I can't remember.
- I don't want to remember.
- I hate my life.
- Bad things happen to me.
- My life is not worth living.
- I am guilty of _____.
- No one likes me.
- I always get left out.
- People betray me.
- People are all phonies.
- People don't tell the truth.
- I am abandoned.
- I would rather be anywhere else than in my body.
- I am alone.
- I need to be invisible to be safe.
- I need to go where no one recognizes me.
- I don't like people.
- I want to be alone.
- If I remember, I will hurt.
- I can't let go of my pain and guilt.
- I can't forgive.
- I can't move on.

- I am worthless.
- I'm not good enough.
- I attract only false friends.

Pineal Gland Calcification

The pineal gland can calcify over time, a process characterized by accumulating calcium and fluoride deposits. These deposits, also known as brain sand, can harden and form phosphate crystals, interfering with the pineal gland's ability to secrete melatonin. Some studies suggest that over 40% of Americans have a calcified pineal gland by their mid-teens.[43,44]

Repeating Patterns

Being unable to let go of what is toxic, can't filter what's not good for them. Poor discretion. Can't evolve. Rejects new concepts. Doesn't listen to their inner voice. Needs are shelved. Wounded Creative Core (see page 123). Victim patterns.

Emotional States

- Shut down hope. Shut down wanting. Shut down their desire for life. The wall of their youth kept them from awareness of their nature. Now that the wall has been breached, they no longer see themselves as reaching for joy or inner peace. They felt disillusioned by all they encountered.

- False hopes and false ideas laid the foundations for despair. The false concepts were the product of institutional control. Joined by others in their disillusionment, they worked to move past the false foundations, and they failed. No support, rejection from family, and harsh judgments about their perceptions.

---

[43] Tan, D. X., Xu, B., Zhou, X., & Reiter, R. J. (2018). Pineal Calcification, Melatonin Production, Aging, Associated Health Consequences and Rejuvenation of the Pineal Gland. *Molecules (Basel, Switzerland)*, *23*(2), 301. Available from https://doi.org/10.3390/molecules23020301

[44] Luke J. (2001). Fluoride Deposition in the Aged Human Pineal Gland. *Caries Research*, *35*(2), 125–128. Available from https://doi.org/10.1159/000047443

- ❖ Aligned forces created an insurmountable objection to their life being lived on their own terms. Forced to comply — they were coerced to be like everyone else and not stick out or be different. Torn between what they knew and what was required conformity, they struggled and contracted.

- ❖ Warm thoughts, ideas of comfort and love turned angry. Life became contracted and harsh. Betrayed and deceived by those they thought loved them. Abandoned. They felt like they could no longer trust.

- ❖ Justice denied. Harsh and violent environment. Wanted someone to pay. Wanted the injustice of powerlessness in the face of violent people rectified. Years of subjugation.

Fears

- ✦ Fear of rejection
- ✦ Fear of abandonment
- ✦ Fear of not being enough
- ✦ Fear of authority
- ✦ Fear of being trapped
- ✦ Fear of injustice
- ✦ Fear of betrayal
- ✦ Fear of trusting
- ✦ Fear of being unloved/unwanted
- ✦ Fear of being happy
- ✦ Fear of peace
- ✦ Fear of having peace
- ✦ Fear of being seen
- ✦ Fear of not staying in line
- ✦ Fear of false hopes
- ✦ Fear of violence
- ✦ Fear of angry people

Created Patterns

- I must submit.
- I must always give in.
- Life is unfair.

- Everything is unfair.
- I get blamed for everything.
- I do what those in authority say.
- I am forced against my will to be something I am not.
- I must stay small to be safe.
- If I am happy, someone takes it away.
- I am hopeless.
- I am depressed.
- I am too old to make my life better.
- Nothing works for me.
- I never get what I want.
- Everything ends up being a disappointment.
- I will never be happy.
- Everybody lies to me.
- I'm not good enough.
- I can't get what I want.
- People tell me what to do.
- I must do what I am told to.
- I can't be myself.
- I can't live my own life.
- I must stay in the shadows.
- I struggle and I fail.
- New ideas lead to disappointment.
- I am abandoned.
- I can't determine when someone is lying to me.
- I'm making no progress in life.
- I seem to fail at everything.
- I can't trust people.
- I don't trust myself.
- I must be sensible.
- I must be reliable at all costs.

Pineal Gland Cysts

A sack of fluid that develops in the pineal gland.[45]

Repeating Patterns

A trauma occurred that could not be dealt with, so it was walled off. Encapsulation of emotional hurt. Wounded creative core. Insecure. Worthless. Unacceptable.

Emotional States

- ❖ There is a wounding related to the creative flow that called for shutting down the sharing of that aspect of self to be safe from inner annihilation.* Emotions are encapsulated to prevent others from seeing the wounds.

    Example: A creative effort was put down, judged, or criticized. That wound causes them to crumple inside. In response, the person no longer shares their creative work. They hide what they do, putting walls around it. They put walls around their feelings about the wound, hence the cyst. Cyst = sac(walls) + fluid (Protection of feelings)

- ❖ Warnings of hatred from another event went unheeded. But were soon realized. They hid the fear of this derangement and carried on as if nothing was wrong, walking on glass and saying nothing was the option.

    Example: This would be in the person's past. Possibly, marriage and the adult stepchildren hated the new wife/husband and told others of that hatred. They were warned of this hatred and ignored the warning. However, in the coming days, hatred became apparent in subsequent interactions.

---

[45] Bosnjak, J., Budisić, M., Azman, D., Strineka, M., Crnjaković, M., & Demarin, V. (2009). Pineal Gland Cysts--an Overview. *Acta Clinica Croatia*, *48*(3), 3 2009 Sep;48(3):355-8. PMID: 20055263. Available from https://pubmed.ncbi.nlm.nih.gov/20055263/

- ❖ Forethought would have saved them from a disastrous event. Reactive response brought them lots of grief. Frozen in the moment of challenge, they could not think and only reacted—harsh and unexpected criticism by another.

- ❖ Living a life of solitude was meant to provide solace but instead created angst. A miscommunication and a misunderstanding. This stopped the flow.

- ❖ Washed over (overwhelmed) by family demands, they had a sense of self-sacrifice for everyone else's needs. This kept them from being seen. This kept them safe. This kept them in control.

Fears

- ✦ Fears being ridiculed
- ✦ Fears rejection
- ✦ Fears being seen as different
- ✦ Fears being vulnerable
- ✦ Fears someone will discover their pain
- ✦ Fear of thinking about their hurt
- ✦ Fears someone will discover their shame
- ✦ Fears invoking the anger of another
- ✦ Fear of not being good enough
- ✦ Fear of being out of sync
- ✦ Fear of being seen
- ✦ Fear of being out of control
- ✦ Fear of being unloved/unaccepted
- ✦ Fear of another's anger
- ✦ Fears making others angry
- ✦ Fears the institutions
- ✦ Fears the control of institutions

Created Patterns

- I must be in control to be safe.
- I must be in control to be safe from myself.
- I am in danger when other people are angry.
- If I am rejected, I am unloved/unwanted/unneeded.

- I can't ever say the right thing.
- I must keep the secrets.
- I feel like I am always walking on glass, so I don't say or do the wrong thing.
- If I am seen as different, I am rejected/unwanted/unloved.
- If I am seen as different, I am discounted as worthless.
- I must control what people say about me.
- People who are angry hurt me.
- I'm not good enough.
- I'm not worthy.
- I am not safe in the institutions (education, religion, corporate, government).
- I am attacked for who I am.
- My value is questioned by others.
- I am diminished when people question who I am.
- I say and do the wrong thing when around others.
- I am not safe from my thoughts.

Pineal Gland Tumor

Pineal gland tumors are growths of abnormal cells; they are not always cancerous. However, they become problematic if they grow to a size that impairs the functioning of adjacent organs.[46]

Repeating Patterns

Overrun by others: their ideas, their actions, their needs. Lack of control and or out-of-control. Powerless to stop people from overrunning them. Shortsightedness. Anger at not being able to stop being overrun. Must take what is given and can't stop what is not good for them.

Emotional States

- ❖ False hope of a better future, a better condition for all of humanity, has led them into depression and angst as they realized this would not be the state of the world.

- ❖ Short-sighted inspiration failed to meet expectations along with false hopes that crash landed in their lap. They froze for fear of being held accountable for their failure. They felt pushed against a wall with no escape and nowhere to go — trapped.

- ❖ False hopes led them down a dark and fraught path with betrayals. Hard lessons. Hard feelings. Hurt by many people.

- ❖ Head-on collision with those who desire to control them and their need to determine their destiny. Continual struggle for their autonomy. Money at its core. Guilt is used to control them. Love is weaponized.

---

[46] Kashani, Shayan(2022). What to Know About Pineal Tumors. Available from
https://www.webmd.com/brain/what-to-know-about-pineal-tumors

Fears

- ✦ Fears people
- ✦ Fear of receiving
- ✦ Fear of being loved
- ✦ Fear of being trapped
- ✦ Fear of being overrun
- ✦ Fear of losing themselves
- ✦ Fear of being obligated
- ✦ Fears people will hurt them
- ✦ Fears being betrayed
- ✦ Fears flow
- ✦ Fears nothing will change for the better
- ✦ Fears change
- ✦ Fears feeling compassion
- ✦ Fears failing
- ✦ Fears being tricked
- ✦ Fears being trapped
- ✦ Fears being cornered
- ✦ Fears being overrun
- ✦ Fears of seeing the outcome of actions
- ✦ Fears knowing

Created Patterns

- People betray me.
- I don't want people giving me things.
- Gifts are an obligation.
- Gifts are an opportunity for people to hurt me.
- Gifts are an opportunity for people to take from me.
- People turn gifts into hate.
- People hurt me.
- People I trust hurt me.
- Anything different is a danger.
- I am taken advantage of.
- Life is always going to be bad.
- Life is hard.
- Change is dangerous.
- When things change, they are out of control.

- When change happens, I feel overrun.
- I am a failure.
- I am powerless.
- It's hopeless.
- Nothing will ever be any better.
- I can't allow things to just happen; I must control them.
- Civilization is doomed.
- I have no hope that things will get any better.
- We are all doomed.
- I don't want people getting close to me.

Pineocytoma

A pineocytoma is a rare, slow-growing pineal gland tumor or mass of abnormal cells that grow in the pineal gland.[47]

Repeating Patterns

Co-dependent. Wounded Creative Core. Hangs on to what is toxic but doesn't know what's toxic. Manipulated and controlled by others.

Emotional States

- ❖ Forced behavior created strong feelings of being forced against their will and trapped with no escape. Someone close to them had gained information that reflected their vulnerability. They used that information to force them against their will to obey, conform, and comply.

- ❖ Closed off from the wounding. They carry the wounds in a secreted place (that means they have stuck them away where they are not visible to others). They believe that if they keep the secret, they won't have to confront the wounds. Confrontation has taught them they will be hurt again.

- ❖ Wrong people and wrong ideas led them astray. They were then ridiculed. Anger and hatred turned toward those that ridiculed them with no letting go — held it in.

- ❖ Others in their life would give and then take back. The person could not seem to learn how they were being controlled as they kept playing the control drama. By staying connected to the control drama, they felt loved and wanted.

---

[47] Fakhran, S., & Escott, E. J. (2008). Pineocytoma Mimicking a Pineal Cyst on Imaging: True Diagnostic Dilemma or a Case of Incomplete Imaging? *AJNR. American Journal of Neuroradiology, 29*(1), 159–163. Available from https://doi.org/10.3174/ajnr.A0750

Fears

- ✦ Fears being trapped
- ✦ Fears of not having free will
- ✦ Fears being forced against their will
- ✦ Fears being found out
- ✦ Fears of having their secrets exposed
- ✦ Fears being vulnerable
- ✦ Fears letting go
- ✦ Fears being destroyed
- ✦ Fears becoming nothing
- ✦ Fears rejection
- ✦ Fears being alone
- ✦ Fear of being lost
- ✦ Fears having to face their wounds
- ✦ Fears hurting
- ✦ Fears being confronted
- ✦ Fears being exposed
- ✦ Fears angry people
- ✦ Fears of being ridiculed/humiliated/shamed

Created Patterns

- I can't leave.
- I can't get away.
- I am trapped.
- I need to run away.
- Nothing I do will make things better.
- I am angry at _____.
- I am forced against my will.
- I have secrets that hurt me.
- I am the victim.
- I am lost.
- I don't know when someone has bad intent toward me.
- Angry people are dangerous.
- I am shameful.
- People ridicule me.
- People shame me.

- People humiliate me.
- I don't know how to react when I am emotionally hurt, so I shut down.
- I am in control by being controlled.
- I would be devastated if others found out my secrets.
- I have no free will.
- I only want what others want.
- I must hide to be safe.
- If I am destroyed, I will starve.
- I have no understanding of peace.
- When I am giving something, it is either destroyed or taken back.

Seasonal Affective Disorder

Seasonal affective disorder (SAD), also known as winter depression, is a type of depression that occurs at certain times of the year, most often in the fall and winter. Studies suggest that reduced sunlight may trigger a chemical change in the brain, leading to symptoms of depression.[48]

Repeating Patterns

Hopeless, withdrawal, guilt, no discernment, no connection to their inner wisdom, don't trust their filters.

Emotional States

- ❖ False ideas. False hopes. False info. This falseness puts them in a place of not knowing what was true, wrong, or right. They froze. Unable to move. Unable to make a decision. Unable to give or receive. They let it all fall apart. Gentleness that was harm. They did not see this coming. (Example: Parent says, "I love you," and then they hurt you.)

- ❖ A joke went sideways. They were left with an impossible mess on their hands. Desperate pleas for help went unanswered. No one felt they needed to help. The mess spiraled out of control, leaving them feeling guilty.

- ❖ Short-sighted memories with no content held them entranced — the shiny object. They felt a sense of false peace and safety when they held those memories in the present. They do this to escape the present, where there is no escape to peace. The present hurts. Silent people dominate their life. There is no connection (heart). These silent people do not acknowledge their presence or their need for humanity. They are cold and distant, silent people.

---

[48] Wikipedia contributors. (2023, April 10). Seasonal Affective Disorder. *Wikipedia, The Free Encyclopedia*. Available from
https://en.wikipedia.org/w/index.php?title=Seasonal_affective_disorder&oldid=1149118093

- ❖ Jolt from a life of reverie — no real substance, they are harshly connected back into the meanness (can mean many things: poverty, people, environment) of their existence. This is an existence of drudgery and struggle. They don't know they can escape.

Fears

- ✦ Fears looking at their shadow
- ✦ Fear of facing their truth
- ✦ Fear of silence
- ✦ Fear of rejection
- ✦ Fear of being unloved/unloved/unwanted
- ✦ Fear of knowing
- ✦ Fear of making a decision
- ✦ Fear of being responsible
- ✦ Fear of being out of control
- ✦ Fear of being in control
- ✦ Fear of flow
- ✦ Fear of allowing
- ✦ Fear of receiving
- ✦ Fear of giving
- ✦ Fear of people who love you
- ✦ Fear of being hurt by people who love you
- ✦ Fear of being unsupported
- ✦ Fear of being unacceptable
- ✦ Fear of the present
- ✦ Fear of what is unsaid
- ✦ Fear of impending doom
- ✦ Fear of breaking out of the abuse
- ✦ Fear that the world is just as bad as their existence, so why change
- ✦ Fear of freedom

Created Patterns

- I am not good enough.
- I am worthless.
- I can't tell when people are lying to me.
- I make bad decisions with bad people.

- I need to hide to be safe.
- I have no hope that things will ever be better.
- I am unrecognized.
- I am out of control.
- I have no control.
- I must stay in control.
- My life will never be any better.
- I am guilty of _____.
- I live my life in guilt.
- Even if I am not guilty, I am guilty.
- I will never be enough.
- People reject me.
- I am unsupported.
- I can't rely on anyone to help me when I need help.
- I am all alone.
- If I give, I will be taken advantage of.
- If I give, people only expect more.
- Receiving will only cause problems.
- If I am free, I will have no one.
- If I leave the abuse, it will just be the same and maybe worse.
- People don't tell me the truth.
- People say mean things to me to hurt me.
- I am unacceptable.
- People that love me hurt me.
- I must stay in control to be safe.
- If I make a decision, I will be wrong, and then I will be hurt.
- Being responsible is dangerous.

Appendix C: Physical Diseases and Disorders Associated with an Impaired Pineal Gland and the Emotional Patterns

Pineal gland calcification results in a lowering of melatonin production. This chapter explores the emotional patterns of diseases where research has implicated lower melatonin levels as having contributed to the development of a disease.[49]

---

[49] Tan, D. X., Xu, B., Zhou, X., & Reiter, R. J. (2018). Pineal Calcification, Melatonin Production, Aging, Associated Health Consequences and Rejuvenation of the Pineal Gland. *Molecules (Basel, Switzerland), 23(2), 301*. Available from https://doi.org/10.3390/molecules23020301

Alzheimer's Disease

Alzheimer's disease causes memory loss and a marked decline in cognitive abilities. Calcification of the pineal gland causes a reduction in melatonin production, which contributes to the development of Alzheimer's disease.[50,51]

Repeated Patterns

Lack of inner peace, cycles thoughts of hatred and feelings of injustice, creates a life of struggle, blames others for their failures, stuck to thoughts and behaviors dictated by institutions, loss of authority, doesn't allow flow, must be in control, no trust, no joy, can't forgive, gets angry when there is change, feels powerless to make changes, judgmental.

Emotional States

- ❖ Longtime hatred of established ways has built resentment deep within the thoughts. This animosity is a result of cultural mores that dictate behavior. They have "obeyed" the cultural mores but held an unsaid and, for the most part, deep resentment toward these mores. Church, institution, family, etc., have said they "must" be this, or they must do that or feel that.

- ❖ Unsaid words holding deep directions (Clarification: Information from the soul) not taken (ignored). Hollow acquiescence to life. The penalty is too high for them to be otherwise. It's too hard to know that they have not answered the deep primal yearnings of their cells.

---

[50] Song, J. Pineal Gland Dysfunction in Alzheimer's Disease: Relationship with the Immune-Pineal Axis, Sleep Disturbance, and Neurogenesis. *Mol Neurodegeneration 14, 28 (2019)*. Available from https://doi.org/10.1186/s13024-019-0330-8

[51] Mahlberg, R., Walther, S., Kalus, P., Bohner, G., Haedel, S., Reischies, F. M., Kühl, K. P., Hellweg, R., & Kunz, D. (2008). Pineal Calcification in Alzheimer's Disease: an In Vivo Study Using Computed Tomography. *Neurobiology of Aging, 29*(2), 203–209. Available from https://doi.org/10.1016/j.neurobiolaging.2006.10.003

- ❖ Warnings from others went unheeded. Hateful speech (bigotry, racism, misogyny, etc.) raced through their being. Remnants of a legacy left in the DNA* with no home, no landing place. Confusion. Words unfelt floating to the surface of awareness. Ancestral DNA finds no resting place in this life.

  Note: Our DNA carries chemical tags attached to a specific place on a DNA strand. Those tags will influence the expression of DNA. From epigenetics research, these tags appear created when great stress or trauma occurs.

  "Epigenetics is the study of how your behaviors and environment can cause changes that affect the way your genes work. Unlike genetic changes, epigenetic changes are reversible and do not change your DNA sequence but can change how your body expresses a DNA sequence."[52]

- ❖ Failure. Life has been a series of failures that have led to biased opinions toward others. Strong sense that others have failed them instead of having failed and taking responsibility for those failures.

- ❖ Hard-won victories over obstacles have created bitterness at the ease of others (others have it easier). They don't realize they have created the obstacles. They pontificate about their hard life and that others should suffer the way they do/have.

- ❖ Justice denied. Feels deep resentment. These are resentments of the mind. Holds negative attitudes that create a maelstrom of anxiety in and around them. They hold things tight to their chest because they fear revealing too much of themselves for fear of being "ripped off" and justice denied again. This resentment is a loop. The pattern repeats in their life.

- ❖ There is a watery aspect of their nature. The water is an overflow of emotions. They will retain water and have issues with edema and other illnesses that reflect a buildup of fluids. The emotions are overwhelming, and they don't know how to express them, so they build up and get reflected in wet maladies.

---

[52] Centers for Disease Control and Prevention. (2022, August 15). What is Epigenetics?. Centers for Disease Control and Prevention. Available from https://www.cdc.gov/genomics-and-health/about/epigenetic-impacts-on-health.html?CDC_AAref_Val=https://www.cdc.gov/genomics/disease/epigenetics.htm

- ❖ Strong emotions of hatred and a lack of fulfillment in their life. A deep sadness fills their being, and the past is mired in sadness. Wrong impressions created sadness. Communication that went awry tumbled over and over in their mind until it became hatred.

- ❖ Falsehoods brought them to a place of not identifying with the life they had built for themselves. When they realized the falsehoods, they disconnected from life. They didn't know how to hit the reset button on their life and create a new way. It was all or nothing.

- ❖ Their shortcomings set up a feeling that they were never going to fit in or be good enough. Their guilt at being less than was overwhelming. At times their guilt over shadowed their ability to live a connected life.

- ❖ The hurts from life became too much. Thinking hurts. Remembering hurt. The awareness of pain made them want to forget and not connect with what made them recall the pain.

- ❖ The pain of life haunted them. It was like a ghost that trailed them everywhere. There was no peace. Every thought was trailed by the non-peace. They did not know how to find peace. All they wanted was to stop the painful thoughts -- thoughts that caused their heart to clinch.

Fears

- ✦ Fear of tomorrow
- ✦ Fear of institutions
- ✦ Fear of being trapped
- ✦ Fear of being forced against their will
- ✦ Fear of giving in
- ✦ Fear of being told what to do
- ✦ Fear of their anger
- ✦ Fear of being out of time
- ✦ Fear of being seen as a failure
- ✦ Fear of being diminished
- ✦ Fear of letting go
- ✦ Fear of being ripped off
- ✦ Fear of being hurt

- ✦ Fear of being out of control
- ✦ Fears being attacked
- ✦ Fears being misunderstood
- ✦ Fear of having their identity challenged
- ✦ Fears of losing their identity
- ✦ Fear of knowing the truth
- ✦ Fear of being lied to
- ✦ Fear of knowing self
- ✦ Fear of not being good enough
- ✦ Fear of change
- ✦ Fear of being unwanted
- ✦ Fear of not fitting in
- ✦ Fear of being different
- ✦ Fear of not conforming and complying
- ✦ Fear of remembering the pain

Created Patterns

- I am angry at _____.
- I am depressed.
- I am going to be hurt by others.
- I am helpless.
- I am helpless to change things.
- I am overwhelmed.
- I am powerless.
- I am powerless to change things.
- I can't be angry at _____.
- I can't cope with life.
- I can't face life anymore.
- I can't let go of the past.
- I don't trust myself.
- I have been overrun.
- I'm not in control of my life.
- I'm not supported.
- It is hopeless.
- It is safer being in my world.
- It's easier to be somewhere else.
- Life is overwhelming.

- My life is being taken away from me.
- My life is out of control.
- Other people must tell me what to do.
- People don't trust me.
- The truth hurts.
- People lie to me.
- People use the truth to hurt me.
- Thinking outside the box will hurt me.
- Change is dangerous.
- I'm not good enough.
- I'm not wanted.
- I must conform to what others want.
- Remembering the past hurts too much.
- I don't fit in.
- People exclude me from their lives.
- Being different is wrong.
- I am guilty of everything.
- When I disconnect I am safe.

Anxiety

Anxiety is the body's response to stress. A person experiencing anxiety may have intense fear, restlessness, apprehension and worry. Low melatonin levels contribute to the development of anxiety. [53,54]

Repeated Patterns

Depression, not honoring the journey, lack of inner peace, ignoring the inner voice of intuition, doesn't trust themselves, painting themselves into a spiritual corner, and does not adapt to life's changes.

Emotional States

- ❖ Can't reconcile the inside with the outside…spiritual with the physical. The physical world (material) creates an inner tension when this person gets too close to the awareness of the higher self.

- ❖ Fear of the pain of failure. Influence of others puts pressure on the person to act in a way different from their inner guidance. This person knows their needs are not being met. They have a feeling of failure when their own needs are not being met. They feel trapped and do not feel like they can change.

- ❖ There is a feeling of overwhelm and that they are in a deep, dark pit. The tools they have used in the past are no longer working. They feel nothing is making their circumstances better. The harder they work at trying to change things through the use of the creative-intuitive or nurturing, the worse their condition seems to get. This state may be reflective of the individual being in a parenting situation

---

[53] National Institute of Mental Health (April 2023). Anxiety Disorder. U.S. Department of Health and Human Services, National Institutes of Health, National Institute of Mental Health. Available from https://www.nimh.nih.gov/health/topics/anxiety-disorders

[54] Association for the Advancement of Restorative Medicine (n.d.). Pineal Disorders: Melatonin Deficiency and Excess. AARM. Available from https://restorativemedicine.org/fundamentals-naturopathic-endocrinology/pineal-disorders-melatonin-deficiency-excess/.

that is frustratingly difficult. They feel trapped, and there is no way out.

- ❖ What has supported this person is now wrapped in uncertainty. They are faced with having to make choices. Everything they know, their foundation, is now reflecting inconsistencies. Their means of self-expression has been shredded. What they have learned now appears rigid and hard. Response to their needs feels cold and mechanical. They feel very alone and unsupported. There is no real place for them to go to feel support from someone else…that is what they see and feel. They have lost sight of love and tolerance of self. This person is not allowing the power of intuition and self-trust to move them through this life transition. There is a fear of looking at the alternatives. All that they have relied on is not there, so they revert to confusion.

- ❖ The first broken heart is the source of anxiety. The first broken heart is when the one they love most in the world hurts them and breaks their trust. They then replicate that pattern of not being worthy of love, never allowing themselves to love.

- ❖ The experience of anxiety is the heart trying to send a message or information. The person in their separation from knowing their heart has suppressed messages from the heart.

Fears

- ✦ Fear that life has too many expectations and they will fail
- ✦ Fears self
- ✦ Fear of intuition
- ✦ Fear of being present
- ✦ Fear of god
- ✦ Fear of failure
- ✦ Fear of things not getting better
- ✦ Fear of being overwhelmed
- ✦ Fear of doing
- ✦ Fear being trapped
- ✦ Fear of uncertainty
- ✦ Fear of being alone

- ✦ Fear of being unsupported
- ✦ Fear of change
- ✦ Fear of love
- ✦ Fears the heart

Created Patterns

- Change is dangerous.
- Change isn't safe.
- Bad things are going to happen to me.
- Decisions are dangerous.
- Everything falls apart.
- Everything is a mess.
- I am alone.
- I am angry at _____.
- I am bitter toward _____.
- I am depressed.
- I am dying.
- I am helpless.
- I am jealous of _____.
- I am lost.
- I am overwhelmed.
- I am trapped.
- I am unsupported.
- I can't change anything.
- I can't depend on anyone or anything.
- I can't let go of _____ (what will happen if you do?).
- I can't move.
- I can't wait for the solutions.
- I don't belong.
- I don't know where to turn.
- I don't know who I am.
- I don't love myself.
- I don't trust myself.
- I don't trust others.
- I expect more from myself than others.
- I give my power away.

- I have no choices.
- I must be better than others.
- I must have things now.
- I want to die.
- I'm not empowered.
- I'm not important to god.
- I'm not in my power.
- I'm not protected.
- I'm not safe.
- I'm not secure.
- I'm stuck.
- If I make a decision, I will get hurt.
- If I make a decision, it will be wrong.
- My intuition has failed me before.
- No one cares about me.
- No one listens to me.
- No one loves me.
- No one understands me.
- Nothing I do works.
- There is no one to help me.
- There is no way out.
- Using my intuition is unreliable.

Depression

Depression is a mental condition characterized by severe sadness and melancholy, typically with feelings of not being good enough and guilt, often accompanied by a lack of energy and disturbance of appetite and sleep. Studies have shown that people with depression often have lower levels of melatonin than people without depression. Lower melatonin levels suggest that decreased production of melatonin may be a contributing factor to depression.[55,56,57]

Repeated Patterns

Wounded Creative Core, loss of identity, abandonment, feeling unaccepted, not allowing, lack of balance, burnout, denial, ego, fear of feeling, lack of flow, lack of forgiveness, ungiving, grief, insecurity, no joy, not letting go, overwhelm, no peace, resentment, trapped, not being their authentic self, unmet needs (no recognition, unloved, disrespected, not being listened to, no support and encouragement), shame, self-denial, broken heart, stuck creativity, denial, trouble receiving, stress, untrusting, unworthiness.

Emotional States

- ❖ A sense that it is hopeless; no one understands or cares. Their insecurity has drained life force. The ability to give and receive has been stopped. Self-worth tied up in outward appearances.

- ❖ Apathetic toward life (Anger turned inward)

---

[55] Sawchuk, Craig MD (2022). What is Depression? Mayo Clinic Available from https://www.mayoclinic.org/diseases-conditions/depression/symptoms-causes/syc-20356007.

[56] Zhao, W., Zhu, D. M., Zhang, Y., Zhang, C., Wang, Y., Yang, Y., Bai, Y., Zhu, J., & Yu, Y. (2019). Pineal Gland Abnormality in Major Depressive Disorder. *Psychiatry Research. Neuroimaging*, 289, 13–17. Available from https://www.sciencedirect.com/science/article/abs/pii/S0925492718303408

[57] Won, E., Na, K.-S., & Kim, Y.-K. (2021). Associations between Melatonin, Neuroinflammation, and Brain Alterations in Depression. *International Journal of Molecular Sciences*, 23(1), 305. Available from https://doi.org/10.3390/ijms23010305

❖ Unexpressed grief from loss.

❖ Quickly judges a situation and moves into a new situation that is really the same (relationships, jobs, geography, etc.). When they finally see the illusion, they have created, they go into a holding pattern and do nothing.

❖ Suppression of inner needs to comply with societal/cultural/family expectations. Fears the loss of love and support if they lead an authentic life. Feels misunderstood.

❖ There is a sense that it is hopeless to express needs and feelings. No one really understands. This individual feels lost, and all attempts at expressing needs are felt to be a waste of time. This person does not know where to turn, and they feel like they are wandering in a space of insecurity. There is a lack of support that makes them feel hopeless. The creative, nurturing, intuitive aspect of self is being overshadowed by a fear based in insecurity. This feeling has drained their life force. This person lashes out at those that are trying to help and refuses to receive (assistance, love, compassion, or support) from others and, in the process, deprecates (belittles) themselves. The energies of the masculine and feminine are out of balance. They are not able to give and receive in a holistic way. Their physical appearance has been a source of objectification via stereotypical assumptions as to intelligence and worth. For example, a physically attractive woman is objectified for her beauty and is considered not very bright. Her entire concept of self-worth is tied up in her outward appearance. This is a trap that she does not know how to get out of. Any movement out of that stereotyped role is thwarted by the people around her; she is only seen as one thing and one thing only. She is constantly reminded of this by her social environment.

❖ This person has taken multiple jumps in new directions in a way that reflects no forethought as to the outcome. They have entered a new situation (relationship, job, venture, geography, etc.), looking for something that they think they are missing. They quickly judge the new situation and move out of it quickly. The judgment is based on a childlike basis of decision-making. There was an aspect of self that, as a child, was left incomplete. This has been their history. Then, one day, they took one of these 'jumps' in a new direction and saw the outcome of this new move. They 'saw' that it was very much the same as the other moves in their life. So, instead of moving into the new situation and working through the lessons of life to be found there, they pulled themselves up above the situation and moved into a place of stasis. They don't know what to do at this point. They are suspended above the life situation. This act of stasis will or has triggered a dark night of the soul.

- This person has experienced a loss of power (relationship, job, life situation, etc.), and they are suppressing the pain of that loss. Unexpressed grief is the thread of emotion throughout their being. The individual is being torn between the values of two different worlds. One of these worlds has very rigid and structured societal expectations that must be complied with, or there are harsh penalties. This person's inner world is in direct contradiction with this societal expectation. So, they suppress their true inner needs and put on an outward appearance of compliance. But, inside, there is a quiet desperation being played out that does not appear to have a solution. If they play out their needs, they will lose what they perceive as a source of support and love. This person feels like no one understands them. They have a masculine energy in their life that is trying to 'fix' this person's unhappiness. That act is actually causing the psychic pain to increase because the masculine energy is going after the wrong thing. The person then withdraws even more into the darkness to hide from the 'fix-it' attempt.

Fears

- Fear of there being no purpose to life
- Fear that what is real is all an illusion
- Fear of life flow
- Fear of being hopeless
- Fear of their anger
- Fear of recognizing loss
- Fear of being nothing
- Fear of the creative core
- Fear of being authentic
- Fear of expressing emotions

- ✦ Fear of being overrun
- ✦ Fear of intrusion
- ✦ Fear of receiving
- ✦ Fear of being trapped
- ✦ Fear of being wrong
- ✦ Fear of being found and seen
- ✦ Fear of doing anything
- ✦ Fear of losing their identity
- ✦ Fear of powerlessness
- ✦ Fear of being unsupported

Created Patterns

- Change isn't safe.
- I always get hurt in relationships.
- I am afraid that I will be criticized.
- I am always being criticized.
- I am annoyed at _____.
- I am not in control.
- I am overwhelmed by change.
- I can't be free to be me.
- I can't cope with the changes happening.
- I can't make a decision and stick with it.
- I can't take it all in.
- I can't talk about my feelings.
- I choke on my feelings.
- I don't seem to have a say in anything.
- I don't understand my feelings.
- I doubt myself.
- I expect myself to be better than others.
- I have high expectations of myself.
- I make decisions quickly, and then I regret what I have done.
- I must always have the answers.
- I must control what I feel; otherwise, I will _____ (be hurt/make a bad decision/ let someone down/ be let down/ be disobedient/ not honor my parents).
- I must criticize myself before someone else does.
- I must find my mistakes before others find them.

- I must judge myself before others judge me.
- I need recognition to be wanted/loved/honored/respected.
- I'm not appreciated.
- I'm not good enough.
- I'm not loved.
- I'm not recognized.
- If I say what I feel, I will be hurt/made fun of/rejected/criticized.
- If I stand my ground, I will be hurt.
- Life is choking me.
- Love hurts.
- My feelings betray me.
- My feelings confuse me.
- Nothing I ever do is right.
- Relationships never work out for me in the long run.
- What is causing the nervousness?
- What is the hesitation?
- I don't want to feel.
- Feeling hurts.
- It hurts to feel.
- I am depressed.
- I don't know what joy is.
- I don't know what joy feels like.
- It's no use.
- Things are beyond my control.
- I'll never be able to be enough, can never do enough
- Life is too painful.
- I am powerless to change.
- I am a failure.
- I am afraid I will fail.
- It is hopeless.
- I am helpless to change things.
- I want to die.
- It's useless.
- I give up.
- I am angry at _____.
- I've wasted my life.
- I make all the wrong choices.

- I should have (what 'should have' is limiting your life).
- I am weak.
- I must be what everyone else wants me to be.
- I am only loved for my beauty.
- I get love by being beautiful.
- I am only loved because of _____.
- I am only love when I do for others.
- I don't know how to love myself.
- I don't know what it feels like to love myself.
- I hate myself.
- I am worthless.
- I am in a dark night of the soul.
- There is no place for me to turn.
- God has abandoned me.
- I am abandoned by _____.
- I feel sorry for myself.
- I must do what others tell me to do, or I will be hurt.
- I can't meet people's expectations.
- People expect too much from me.
- I am lost.
- I have no direction.
- Things will never get better, so I may as well die.
- I am angry.

Depression with a History of Abuse

A substantial body of evidence suggests that childhood trauma can play a significant role in the development of depression. Additionally, studies have shown that adults abused as children often have disrupted sleep patterns. Lower melatonin levels suggest that decreased production of melatonin may be a contributing factor to depression.[58,59,60,61]

Repeating Patterns

They have many illnesses because their body is disconnected from their mind and heart. They use drugs to cope. Relationships are surface only, and when they begin to fall apart, the person will run — applies to career, school, intimate partners, and children. Will have injuries or illness and does not really experience discomfort.

Emotional States

- ❖ Hopelessness creates a sense of separation and when one feels separated from their body – a feeling that there is no connection to what is happening with the body – this gives rise to an incoherence that yields depression as a symptom – numbness would be a way of surviving a body that is being abused – there is a feeling of duality in the existence. 'I have a body, but I am not part of the body – I am

---

[58] Agorastos, A., & Olff, M. (2020). Traumatic Stress and the Circadian System: Neurobiology, Timing and Treatment of Post Traumatic Chrono Disruption. *European Journal of Psychotraumatology*, 11(1), 1833644. Available from https://doi.org/10.1080/20008198.2020.1833644

[59] Negele, A., Kaufhold, J., Kallenbach, L., & Leuzinger-Bohleber, M. (2015). Childhood Trauma and Its Relation to Chronic Depression in Adulthood. *Depression Research and Treatment*, 2015, 650804. Available from https://doi.org/10.1155/2015/650804.

[60] De Bellis, M. D., & Zisk, A. (2014). The Biological Effects of Childhood Trauma. *Child and Adolescent Psychiatric Clinics of North America*, 23(2), 185–vii.
Available from https://doi.org/10.1016/j.chc.2014.01.002

[61] Bob, P., & Fedor-Freybergh, P. (2008). Melatonin, Consciousness, and Traumatic Stress. *Journal of Pineal Research*, 44(4), 341–347.
Available from https://doi.org/10.1111/j.1600-079X.2007.00540.x

separate and distinct.' Transmutation cannot take place unless there is an awareness of the numbness in the body. The person that has been abused will not stay with a sensation long enough to work through a healing transmutation. They contact a sensation and immediately retreat into numbness and back to separation. Now, they have moved to the head. They acknowledge that there was a feeling, but the feeling moved into the head very quickly – staying numb is survival.

❖ Depression can manifest as sadness, which keeps the person feeling safe. The sadness is the person's identification with life and security. Nurturance was pain, hurt and violation. Lack of nurturance. The sadness keeps a person from the felt sense in the body. So, the sadness keeps others from seeing the real pain of physical violation. The person does not have to feel the pain of the stored trauma in the body. They won't have to feel the terror of living. No one will see the weakness and shame. They have an idea that people will see them as powerful. The thought process being that they will think "I am powerful and not know that I am powerless." This will keep others away and, by default, keep away the pain and hurt. They will be left alone. Being near others brings on overwhelm. Being overwhelmed leads to freezing – terror is freezing. The freezing keeps the memories from being triggered. There is a fear that when they get close to the place of remembering the experience of trauma, the feeling of that trauma (terror, rage, helplessness) will be recreated. An aversion response is stimulated, and the safety in flight response is triggered.

Fears

- ✦ Fear of being forced to be something they're not
- ✦ Fear of being forced to do against their will
- ✦ Fear of hopelessness
- ✦ Fear of being unloved
- ✦ Fear of being unwanted
- ✦ Fear of disconnection
- ✦ Fear of feeling their body
- ✦ Fear of feeling emotions
- ✦ Fear of pain

- ✦ Fear of receiving
- ✦ Fear of living
- ✦ Fear of being powerless
- ✦ Fear of overwhelm
- ✦ Fear of remembering
- ✦ Fear of being terrorized
- ✦ Fear of being hurt
- ✦ Fear of being seen
- ✦ Fear of their anger

Created Patterns

- I am hopeless.
- My heart is numb.
- I don't feel.
- Feelings are dangerous.
- I am alone.
- I am unloved.
- I am unwanted.
- I am powerless.
- I am out of control.
- I must run away to be safe.
- I must freeze to be safe.
- People hurt me.
- I am depressed.
- Being depressed is safety.
- I am weak.
- I am ashamed.
- I am angry at _____.

Huntington's Disease

Huntington's Disease is an inherited disease that causes the deterioration of nerve cells in the brain. Studies show a significant reduction of melatonin in Huntington's disease. This reduction in melatonin levels may be due to several factors, including damage to the pineal gland, disrupted sleep patterns, and increased oxidative stress (see page 240).[62, 63]

Repeating Patterns

Selfish, controlling, rigid, needs to feel important and valuable, opinionated, judgmental, out of balance giving and receiving.

Emotional States

- ❖ Childlike approaches are used to manipulate and control the world around them. Doesn't hear what other people try to tell them in regard to the need to change who they are. Wants people to be subservient to their needs. Wants to be left alone when their needs are not met–sulk. Sulking is used as a way of punishing those that resist the manipulation. High maintenance. Hardened ideas, inflexible, forceful/pushy manner and approach.

- ❖ Freely lets their hardness toward people be known. Doesn't want to know the viewpoint of others. Knows that they can't always have their way and resents it. Resentment builds. Wants to be seen as the center. Needs to be the center; otherwise, they are unhappy. Hangs onto a glory long past.

---

[62] Kalliolia, E., Silajdžić, E., Nambron, R., Hill, N. R., Doshi, A., Frost, C., Watt, H., Hindmarsh, P., Björkqvist, M., & Warner, T. T. (2014). Plasma Melatonin is Reduced in Huntington's Disease. *Movement Disorders: Official Journal of the Movement Disorder Society, 29*(12), 1511–1515. Available from https://doi.org/10.1002/mds.26003

[63] Chen, D., Zhang, T., & Lee, T. H. (2020). Cellular Mechanisms of Melatonin: Insight from Neurodegenerative Diseases. Biomolecules, 10(8), 1158. Available from https://doi.org/10.3390/biom10081158

- ❖ Heartfelt desire to not be needed by others wants to be free of restrictions imposed on them by others. Does not allow others to exist or be without judging them. Collapses under the weight of their judgment and decisions. Rigid attitudes about others. Feels people should get out of their way. Heart is walled off from the support and kindness of others in a reciprocal fashion. Jumps into the fire of controversy to be the center of attention. Few people want to be around them because of their way of being in the world. Feeds off the energy of others.

- ❖ The natural distinction between right and wrong is distorted. Confuses the principles of right and wrong. Thinks that right and wrong can be manipulated for their advantage. The concept of honor is lost. Patterning comes from parental behavior. Heart is tender and easily wounded when values are exposed as being out of sync with societal expectations.

Fears

- ✦ Fear of being forced to reveal their secrets
- ✦ Fears someone might need something from them
- ✦ Fears the box
- ✦ Fears being out of control
- ✦ Fears being controlled by others
- ✦ Fears the assumptions about who they are
- ✦ Fears being judged
- ✦ Fears being ignored
- ✦ Fears not being adored
- ✦ Fears change
- ✦ Fears becoming nothing
- ✦ Fears disappearing

Created Patterns

- Everything must be done my way.
- Change is dangerous.
- I deeply resent _____.
- My life is hopeless.

- I might as well die; it's hopeless.
- Death would be preferable to living any longer.
- I am always right and don't need the opinions of others.
- I want to die.
- I can't change things, so I might as well die.
- I have no control.
- People ignore me.
- I have to get people's attention somehow.
- I must make people pay attention to me.
- I am helpless to make a change.
- I am a victim.
- I have lost everything.
- Everything good is taken away from me.
- It was easier being a kid.
- I want to go back to being a kid.
- Kids have it so much easier.
- I expect people to do as I say.
- I expect people to listen and do as I say.
- The world becomes unsafe when things don't work out as I planned.
- I am in danger.
- It doesn't do any good to explain things to people.
- No one cooperates with me.
- I must get people's attention to be listened to.
- I must punish others who don't do as I say.
- I must punish others that don't listen to me.
- People are stupid.
- People must be told what to do.
- Things were better when _____.
- People take from me.
- I don't want to support others.
- I decide what is right or wrong.
- Other people are wrong.
- I must use others before they use me.
- If I am wrong, I will be hurt.
- It's every man for himself.
- I am always wrong.
- I'm not good enough.

- I can't have people depending on me.
- Responsibility is bad.
- I can't let go.
- If I let go of the past then I will be hurt again.
- People never mean what they say.
- I can't forgive and forget.
- I hate myself.

Insomnia

Melatonin facilitates the regulation of the sleep-wake cycle. People with insomnia often have low melatonin levels, which can contribute to their sleep problems.[64]

Repeating Patterns

Disconnected, haunted by the past, guilt, shame, PTSD, not good enough, anxiety, hyper-alert, and depression.

Emotional States

- ❖ Witless, does not understand they are here for a reason, and they are not reflecting on the nature of their beingness. Mind is reactive and plows through life. Shows up at a job, gets married, has a family, all without introspection and understanding their nature. The higher self demands their awareness as they try to fall asleep.

- ❖ Hard to know what or where they find a motivational purpose. Unfounded annoyances keep them up and upset their tummy. They don't feel or sense a higher purpose or direction.

- ❖ Pain becomes all-consuming. A small ache becomes huge and creates discomfort. The pain is a distraction from the space and quiet of sleep. For within the quiet of pre-sleep are memories that create angst.

- ❖ Sleeping is dangerous. When they sleep, they feel vulnerable to attack. Bad things happen to them in their sleep. They must make sure everything is safe. They can't let anyone die in the night. They need to be on guard to protect others. They must protect the babies.

---

[64] Zisapel N. (2018). New Perspectives on the Role of Melatonin in Human Sleep, Circadian Rhythms and Their Regulation. *British Journal of Pharmacology, 175(16), 3190–3199.* Available from https://doi.org/10.1111/bph.14116

- ❖ Created pain pattern. There is an awareness of pain in their body when they lie down to go to sleep. A created pain pattern is pain that moves into a person's awareness when triggered by a specific set of external events, like lying down to go to sleep.

Fears

- ✦ Fear of the inner voice
- ✦ Fear of the memories
- ✦ Fear of the future (what might happen next)
- ✦ Fear of stepping outside the box
- ✦ Fear of upsetting the apple cart
- ✦ Fear of feeling
- ✦ Fear of remembering
- ✦ Fear of the night
- ✦ Fear of sleeping
- ✦ Fear of loud noises
- ✦ Fear of attack
- ✦ Fear of being hurt
- ✦ Fear of being different

Created Patterns

- I am guilty of _____.
- I'm not good enough to get the job done.
- I am being threatened by _____.
- I'm not good enough.
- If I stop thinking, something bad will happen.
- The only quiet time to think is right before I go to sleep.
- I am vulnerable when I am sleeping.
- I can never let down my guard.
- The world is not safe.
- I must always be on guard.
- There is no one to protect me.
- I will be hurt when I go to sleep.
- I am afraid of _____.
- I am going to die.
- I must worry at night; I don't get a chance at any other time.

- I have no purpose.
- I have no direction.
- I can't sleep.
- The pain is everything.
- The pain fills my brain.
- I am the pain.
- I don't know where I am going.
- I must worry to keep bad things from happening.
- The pain screams at me at night.
- Finding out the reason for pain is hard; it is easier to take a pill.
- My memories are painful and I would rather not go there.
- Sleeping is dangerous.
- When I sleep, I am vulnerable to attack.
- I need to be on guard to protect others.
- I can't let anyone die in the night.
- I can't turn my brain off.
- When I sleep, I am vulnerable.
- I must keep my guard up.
- There is no one to protect me.
- If I sleep, I will be hurt.
- What is changing or could change in your life?
- I must constantly protect myself.
- I am overloaded.
- I am depressed.

Insulin Resistance

Insulin resistance is when the body's tissues don't respond appropriately to the hormone insulin. Insulin is a hormone that helps the body's cells absorb glucose (sugar) from the blood. When cells become resistant to insulin, they cannot absorb glucose as effectively, which can lead to high blood sugar levels. Studies have shown that melatonin increases insulin receptivity in the cells.[65,66]

Repeating Patterns

Shame, humiliation, weak boundaries, lives in the framework of conform and comply, prevents joy, undeserving, lives by other people's standards, can't receive, can't let go, controlling, no sweetness/joy allowed, disconnected – not present.

Emotional States

- ❖ Held up to others as an example of what they should and shouldn't do. Shame and humiliation are the results. Laughing on the outside but crying on the inside. Joined by others in the laughter and wants to hide. No boundaries – overrun by life and all relationships. Feels depleted with no more to give but keeps giving.

- ❖ They embody an idealized way of being in the world that does not meet reality. Hopes at some point, the world will give way around them and they can stop living the idealized format for existence. Living that way is compulsive. They feel like they have no choices.

---

[65] Ciaran J. McMullan, Gary C. Curhan, Eva S. Schernhammer, John P. Forman Association of Nocturnal Melatonin Secretion With Insulin Resistance in Nondiabetic Young Women *American Journal of Epidemiology, Volume 178, Issue 2, 15 July 2013, Pages 231–238,* Available from https://doi.org/10.1093/aje/kws470

[66] Sharma, S., Singh, H., Ahmad, N., Mishra, P., & Tiwari, A. (2015). The Role of Melatonin in Diabetes: Therapeutic Implications. *Archives of Endocrinology and Metabolism, 59(5), 391–399.* Available from https://doi.org/10.1590/2359-3997000000098

- ❖ Worried about everything around them. They can't let go of the past stuff and that becomes the foundation and justification for the worry. The worry distorts their image of their life reality.

- ❖ Runaway thoughts about life. They can't stop the thinking. It's like a train that just keeps going. There's this outward sense of being in control, but inside, they feel completely out of control.

- ❖ Decreased sense of ownership for the stuff around them – a loss of connection to the world around them – a disconnectedness. There is an emptiness in their movements and a sense of duty-bound functions – they are just going through the motions.

Fears

- ✦ Fear of being publicly shamed
- ✦ Fear of being overrun
- ✦ Fear of receiving
- ✦ Fear of being trapped
- ✦ Fear of the future
- ✦ Fear of thinking
- ✦ Fear of stopping
- ✦ Fear of being present
- ✦ Fear of being hurt

Created Patterns

- I am shamed.
- I am humiliated.
- I am an example of what not to do.
- I must keep a facade.
- I don't deserve.
- I don't know what joy feels like.
- Joy is wrong.
- I must not show people how I truly feel.
- When I laugh, it is false; I want to run away.
- I must give to be wanted/loved/cherished.
- Relationships drain me.

- I have no choices.
- I have to keep up with the Joneses.
- I have to keep up appearances.
- I can't let go.
- I must hang on to be safe
- I worry about everything.
- My mind races, and I can't stop it.
- I am out of control.
- I worry to stay in control.
- I don't belong.
- I am empty.
- I am unconnected.
- Receiving is unsafe.

Lupus

Lupus is a chronic (long-term) disease that can cause inflammation and pain in any part of your body. It's an autoimmune disease, which means that your immune system — the body system that usually fights infections — attacks healthy tissue instead. Studies have shown that people with lupus have low levels of melatonin. Several theories have pointed to low melatonin levels causing an imbalance in the immune system and the body's ability to repair damage.[67, 68, 69]

Repeating Patterns

Food sensitivities, food taste change, sensitivity to the impact of food on their energy system, changes in the digestive system, sensitivity to chemicals and smells, life is always a struggle, lots of setbacks with minimal reward, grief, feeling constrained by the judgment of others, discourages easily, self-sabotage, insecure, bad things always happen to them.

Emotional States

- ❖ This individual has moved into the unknown territory of their unconscious. This individual is dealing with emotions and feelings that they do not understand. They have moved from one committed relationship to another (jobs, friends, spouse/significant other), looking for something that nourishes them. This nourishment is what they need to survive. They are looking to others to fulfill the angst of the unknown.* They feel their life has had many struggles, obstacles and

---

[67] National Resource Center on Lupus(n.d.). What is Lupus? Available from
https://www.lupus.org/resources/what-is-lupus

[68] J.R. Calvo, M.D. Maldonado. The Role of Melatonin in Autoimmune and Atopic Diseases[J]. *AIMS Molecular Science, 2016, 3(2): 158-186.* Available from
https://doi.org/10.3934/molsci.2016.2.158

[69] Robeva, R., Tanev, D., Kirilov, G., Stoycheva, M., Tomova, A., Kumanov, P., Rashkov, R., & Kolarov, Z. (2013). Decreased Daily Melatonin Levels in Women with Systemic Lupus Erythematosus - Short Report. *Balkan Medical Journal, 30(3), 273–276.* Available from
https://doi.org/10.5152/balkanmedj.2013.8064

disappointments. This person has a great deal of personal power. Their words and deeds can be very effective in both a positive and negative fashion. This individual is attracted to the energy of what they are not. They may be in relationships with people that they see as lacking assertiveness. When that person does not give them what they believe they need in the relationship, they will leave. They will use their personal power to overreact to small incidents and use that excuse to leave the relationship. In the process, they may use their powerful verbal skills to diminish the other person further.

Clarification: The angst of the unknown is the anxiety and worry about what might happen. The unknown can be fearful and, in some cases, paralyzing. When there is an unknown and fear, this person projects the fulfillment of that danger being done by "others." Others are the people in their world. For example, in a dysfunctional household, there is constant worry about what might happen. A child knows something bad will happen; they don't know when or what.

- ❖ This person has lost their hope in the midst of despair. This person has either a masculine aspect of self or a masculine presence in their life that is coming in and working to break down 'what they perceive' to be this individual's problems into smaller pieces. This masculine energy is doing what comes naturally wanting to solve the problem. Their efforts are absorbed (transformed) into resentment and hatred as they do this. This negativity (blackness) spills out and absorbs the individual and the foundations that have nourished them. This person perceives their life as being very dark and negative.

- ❖ This person feels as if they have reached a critical point in their life and they are afraid of losing control. They may also feel insecure and a lack of support in their life. These feelings may have their foundation in temptation and guilt. They may feel that they have failed to reach a goal that they set for themselves. They are going through some difficult times, and they are afraid of what is ahead of them. They have been or are involved in deeply painful relationships or unhealthy, destructive behaviors. They see their life in terms of having been full of obstacles and struggles. They feel depressed or strangled by the situation or person. They may be struggling against an obligation or responsibility. This person feels as if they are dying inside. They feel as if the situation is hopeless, and they don't know how to get out of it. This person feeds off old, decaying ideas rather than creative, alive new ones.

❖ Doesn't understand the emotions they are feeling and are looking for a relationship that nurtures them (job, friends, or significant other). If they don't get needs met externally, they leave.

❖ Has lost hope and has feelings of despair. Help from someone trying to help results in resentment and hatred. Sees life as dark and negative.

❖ Afraid of losing control. Feels insecure and a lack of support. Feels like they have failed to reach goals. Afraid of the future. In relationships that are destructive. Feel depressed by a situation or person. Feels like they are dying inside. This person feeds off of what is old and decaying.

❖ They may have an ancestral history of having to keep a secret of shame. That secret is kept in the family and never spoken about or acknowledged.

Fears

- ✦ Fear of hopelessness
- ✦ Fear of heart hurt
- ✦ Fear that their nightmares are in their waking life
- ✦ Fear of their hatred
- ✦ Fear that they are wrong
- ✦ Fear of the unknown
- ✦ Fear of losing control
- ✦ Fear of being forced to be present
- ✦ Fear of hope – loss of identity
- ✦ Fear of the unknown
- ✦ Fear that their darkest secret of shame will be revealed

Created Patterns

- I feel like giving up.
- I am grieving _____.
- I have been holding/feeling strong emotions of anger for a long time.
- What are the boundary issues in your life?
- I must control the world around me.
- I resent _____.
- I can't stop people from _____.
- I have to work hard to please my parents/husband/sister.
- My parents have to be proud of me.
- Failing is fearful/dangerous.
- Failing is the end of the struggle.
- Failing is a sin.
- If I fail, I earn god's anger.
- I can't stand up for myself.
- There's no way out.
- I am disappointed with myself/others…who are the others, and what did they do to disappoint you?
- It would be much easier to die than go on living.
- It would be easier to die than try and change things.
- I have no purpose.
- My life is meaningless.
- Every time I try to do something, I am stopped.
- I will be hurt/ridiculed/shamed/embarrassed if I express my feelings.
- My mother did not protect me.
- I resent/hate/angry at/bitter toward my Mother/Father.
- God abandoned me.
- I am disconnected from god.
- God betrayed me.
- There is no god.
- God is out to get me.
- I am bad/evil.
- I deserve to die for my sins.
- My life is out of control.
- _____ is overwhelming.

- People deserve it when I am angry.
- I deserve to be punished.
- My anger keeps me safe.
- My anger keeps me from getting well.
- I am taken advantage of.
- I must win, or I am worthless.
- I am a failure *(what made you feel that way and what does being a failure mean?)*.
- People always fail me.
- No one ever meets my expectations - they always let me down.
- I can't trust anyone.
- I'm in a no-win situation.
- I am depressed.
- I am angry at _____.
- I don't forgive myself.
- I hurt _____.
- It is hopeless.
- Life is a continual struggle.
- I am forced to _____ *(this person may be the caretaker for someone and they resent having to do that)*.
- I resent _____.
- I hate _____.
- I hate myself.
- I give up.
- Life will never get better.
- Life is hard/a struggle.
- Feelings are dangerous.
- I am shameful.
- My secrets would destroy me.
- I must keep my secrets.

Migraines

A migraine is more than just a bad headache. It is a neurological disease that can cause debilitating throbbing pain, nausea, and other symptoms. The pain can be so severe that it can leave someone in bed for days.[70] Research has shown that pineal calcification may be associated with migraine.[71]

Repeating Patterns

Ancestral trauma of prolonged periods of loss and grief creates emotional changes such as depression. Sense of hopelessness and helplessness are enough to create epigenetic changes that affect serotonin production. An intense fear of loss or grief during the mother's pregnancy affected the serotonin levels of the mother.

Emotional States

- ❖ Inner conflict with being told what to do and knowing that their way would be the best way, but they have to prove the other way wrong. Frustration/anger level is high, and it is turned inward. They don't believe they have the power to express themselves to authority.

- ❖ Fear of being their authentic self. Fear that they are not good enough. Fear of being judged. Fear of being vulnerable. Anxiety when in the spotlight.

---

[70] Amaal Starling, M.D. (2023) What is a Migraine? A Mayo Clinic Expert Explains. Mayo Clinic. Availailable from https://www.mayoclinic.org/diseases-conditions/migraine-headache/symptoms-causes/syc-20360201

[71] Ozlece, H. K., Akyuz, O., Ilik, F., Huseyinoglu, N., Aydin, S., Can, S., & Serim, V. A. (2015). Is there a Correlation Between the Pineal Gland Calcification and Migraine? *European Review for Medical and Pharmacological Sciences, 19(20), 3861–3864* Available from https://pubmed.ncbi.nlm.nih.gov/26531271/

- ❖ Never enough time. The lack of time creates a sense of failure. Failure produces anxiety because they can't meet the expectations of others.

- ❖ Being torn between two worlds, two cultures, competing value systems and demands. They are expected to be one person at work and then be someone else at home and then yet again be someone else in the community or two cultures with concepts or mores that conflict.

- ❖ People in their life reflect back to them their non-acceptance of themselves. They struggle to be comfortable in their skin, and others remind them of that. They attack their appearance, what they say and what they do.

Fears

- ✦ Fear of loss
- ✦ Fear of phantoms (there is a sense that they are carrying the traumas of past ancestors)
- ✦ Fear of authority
- ✦ Fear of being accused of being wrong
- ✦ Fear of showing who they are
- ✦ Fear of letting others down
- ✦ Fear of not meeting expectations
- ✦ Fear of being pulled in different directions
- ✦ Fear of attack
- ✦ Fear of being shown to be less than
- ✦ Fear of the secrets

Created Patterns

- I must take things at my own pace.
- I hate being pushed.
- It is too dangerous to remember.
- Everyone wants a piece of me.
- I am afraid of doing something wrong.
- I am afraid of everything.
- Everything is my fault.

- I can't handle pressure/stress.
- I want control.
- There is never enough time to get things done.
- I can't say no.
- People expect too much from me.
- I must be perfect.
- I must meet people's expectations.
- I am a failure.
- I must do what others tell me to do.
- I don't trust myself.
- I don't trust my intuition.
- I fear the judgment of others.
- I am rejected for who I really am.
- I can't create who I really want to be.
- Being seen is dangerous.
- If I fail, I am not good enough.
- If I am wrong, I will be rejected/not accepted/not loved.
- I'm not good enough.
- I'm not worthy.
- I must prove others wrong to be seen as valuable.
- I must prove others wrong to be right.
- I can't say no.
- I don't have good boundaries.
- I put pressure on myself.
- I am going to die.
- I must hold the secrets.

Motor neuron disease (ALS)

Motor neuron disease is a neurological disease that damages nerves and leads to the wasting of muscles. Studies show a significant reduction of melatonin in ALS. This reduction in melatonin levels may be due to several factors, including damage to the pineal gland, disrupted sleep patterns, and increased oxidative stress (see page 240).[72, 73]

Repeating Patterns

Wounded Creative Core, depression, doesn't let go of stuff that doesn't work – keeps doing the same thing, expecting a different result, a continual sense of failing.

Emotional States

- ❖ Junked ideas pile up in the corners of their life like rotten garbage that has not been taken out. They have not let go of concepts or ideas that they know do not work in their life—fostered concepts in others that will be proven unreliable. Whole areas of their lives look like plains of darkness. They refuse to journey into the darkness and they refuse to clean out piles of junked ideas. They fear falling into the abyss if they let go. They fear dropping into the darkness of the unknown. An ancestral trauma where either choice made would result in death.

- ❖ Feels as if getting anywhere in life is like scaling a vertical cliff of sheer basalt. There is nothing to hang on to, and it is almost impossible to drive a piton into the rock, so they climb. They hardly ever win or accomplish what they set out to do. That is their feeling. Un-

---

[72] Shaw, PJS, Wood-Allum, C (2010). Motor Neurone Disease: a Practical Update on Diagnosis and Management. *Clinical Medicine Journal Jun 2010, 10 (3) 252-258*; Available from https://www.rcpjournals.org/content/clinmedicine/10/3/252

[73] Chen, D., Zhang, T., & Lee, T. H. (2020). Cellular Mechanisms of Melatonin: Insight from Neurodegenerative Diseases. *Biomolecules, 10(8), 1158.* Available from https://doi.org/10.3390/biom10081158

written rules of behavior have kept them constrained. They can only climb that wall one way or not at all. Ancestral trauma: if they go another way or take a different path to the top of the cliff, they will be hurt or die.

Fears

- ✦ Fear of letting go
- ✦ Fear that they have traveled a road to their own doom
- ✦ Fear of changing course
- ✦ Fear of falling
- ✦ Fear of the unknown
- ✦ Fear of accomplishment
- ✦ Fear of the rules

Created Patterns

- No one knows how to listen to me.
- Life is a struggle.
- Life is hard.
- If you don't struggle, it's not worth it.
- Things should never come easy.
- If it's easy, it's not worth anything.
- There's only one way to do things.
- I will die if I stay where I'm at.
- I can't win.
- I can't let go.
- I'm never enough.
- My accomplishments are never enough.
- People don't listen to me.
- I fear change.
- I am paralyzed with fear.
- I have no control of my life.
- Someone has taken my power (who?).
- It is better to concede than fight.
- It's not safe to relax and go with the flow.
- Day by day, I am losing my power.

- People take my power from me.
- The loss of my power is the loss of my life.

Multiple Sclerosis

Multiple sclerosis (MS) is a chronic disease affecting the central nervous system (CNS), which comprises the brain, spinal cord, and optic nerves. In MS, the immune system attacks the myelin sheath, a fatty layer that protects nerve fibers. This damage can slow or block nerve signals, leading to various symptoms.[74] Studies show a significant reduction of melatonin in multiple sclerosis. This reduction in melatonin levels may be due to several factors, including damage to the pineal gland, disrupted sleep patterns, and increased oxidative stress (see page 240).[75]

Repeating Patterns

Invisible, weak boundaries, feel small, change is dangerous, no control or controlling, ungrounded, shame, worthless, unheard, insecure.

Emotional States

- ❖ Disconnection between the needs of the heart and body and what is being told to them by the brain. Overreaction to a perceived violation of boundaries. Epigenetic.

Fears

- ✦ Fear of listening to the heart
- ✦ Fear that they will only see the disease and not me
- ✦ Fear that I will be shamed
- ✦ Fear of listening to the inner self
- ✦ Fear of being overrun

---

[74] Oliver Tobin, M.B., B.Ch., B.A.O., Ph.D. (2022). What is Multiple Sclerosis? An Expert Explains. Mayo Clinic. Available from https://www.mayoclinic.org/diseases-conditions/multiple-sclerosis/symptoms-causes/syc-20350269

[75] Sandyk, R. (1992). The Pineal Gland and the Clinical Course of Multiple Sclerosis. *The International Journal of Neuroscience, 62(1-2), 65–74.* Available from https://doi.org/10.3109/00207459108999758.

- ✦ Fear of being overwhelmed
- ✦ Fear of change
- ✦ Fear of being out of control
- ✦ Fear abandonment

Created Patterns

- Change is dangerous.
- Controlling everything keeps me safe.
- Everyone else gets all the luck.
- God doesn't love me.
- I am afraid of disappointing others.
- I am depressed.
- I am going to die.
- I am guilty of _____.
- I am out of control.
- I am powerless/I have no control/I am dominated.
- I am responsible for _____.
- I am worthless.
- I blame myself for _____.
- I can't communicate.
- I can't forgive myself/others.
- I can't make changes.
- I can't talk to others.
- I can't change.
- I can't take care of myself.
- I don't listen to what others are telling me.
- I don't deserve to heal.
- I hate my mother/father.
- I must be perfect.
- I need someone else to take care of me.
- I shut down my feelings to keep from being hurt.
- I'm not good enough.
- Life is out of control.
- New things are scary/ threatening.
- New things aren't safe.
- Nothing I do is ever enough.

- Others don't hear me.
- Others don't listen to me.

Parkinson's Disease

Parkinson's disease is a progressive neurological disorder that affects movement. A loss of dopamine-producing neurons in the brain causes Parkinson's disease. Dopamine is a chemical messenger that helps control movement. A decrease in dopamine levels can lead to uncontrollable tremors, stiffness, shaking and other symptoms of Parkinson's disease.[76] Research suggests that a drop in melatonin levels may be a risk factor for Parkinson's disease. One study found that people with low melatonin levels were more likely to develop Parkinson's disease than people with normal melatonin levels.[77]

Repeating Patterns

Controlling, guilt, trapped, must be punished, feminine and masculine out of balance, trapped, not allowing flow, untrusting, struggles with the Wounded Creative Core (see page 123).

Emotional States

❖ Masculine aspect of self tries to control those around them; this just leads to failure, with no one wanting to help facilitate that way of being in the world. This person needs to be in control. This need is from an intense fear of failing or falling. So, this intense fear keeps them from making decisions. The more they try to hold on, the less control they have, a loss of power, and this leads to an internal panic. They have held on too tightly and lost their perspective, position, and balance. They see their life as being very difficult and progress has

---

[76] National Institute of Aging (n.d.). Parkinson's disease: Causes, symptoms, and treatments. Available from https://www.nia.nih.gov/health/parkinsons-disease

[77] Mack, J. M., Schamne, M. G., Sampaio, T. B., Pértile, R. A., Fernandes, P. A., Markus, R. P., & Prediger, R. D. (2016). MELATONINERGIC System in Parkinson's Disease: From *Neuroprotection to the Management of Motor and Nonmotor Symptoms. Oxidative Medicine and Cellular Longevity, 2016, 1–31.* Available from https://pubmed.ncbi.nlm.nih.gov/27829983/

been very slow, if not impossible. This person feels unsupported and alone.

❖ There is a feeling of being trapped, and they can't get out. They don't see a way of getting out of the current way of thinking. They believe that the trap they feel themselves in is the making of others. This person feels like there is a whole lot they want to do, but they can't find a way of getting out of the trap they feel they are in. This person has basically put a lid on their inner self so that others could not get near (fear of being hurt) that vulnerable aspect of who they are. This probably happened as a child. That inner child wants to get out and grow into the holistic self. The different aspects of this person's self are kept separate and distinct instead of a blended whole.

❖ Used judgment that then became a deep-abiding guilt. Didn't listen to the inner voices that were telling them to soften; instead, their comfort/discomfort zone took them in a different direction. Thought (ancestral) they were supposed to be that way. Does not trust the inner voice.

❖ Unable to communicate with clarity the needs of the heart to the brain-mind (thinking) and others to be heard. Unable to hang on to what they have and they feel powerless. Their needs get met by being out of control and powerless. They hang onto those around them through manipulation. Life is a struggle of hard disappointments.

❖ False hope, false ideals. They built their foundations on the external, the physical. Their hopes were external and not in their heart. Their view of the future, they believed, would be able to continue on in the way they had been without seeing their true heart and their true essence.

❖ Intense guilt for actions that hurt others with no way of reversing the damage.

Fears

✦ Fear of losing control
✦ Fear of being in control

- ✦ Fear of the unknown
- ✦ Fear that they are living a life that is retribution for their sins
- ✦ Fear of not being able to provide
- ✦ Fear of not being able to do
- ✦ Fear of being trapped
- ✦ Fear of the inner voice
- ✦ Fear of their feminine side (ancestral)
- ✦ Fears loss of power
- ✦ Fear of failure
- ✦ Fear of their heart
- ✦ Fear of being wrong
- ✦ Fear of being guilty
- ✦ Fear of hurting others

Created Patterns

- Failing is not an option.
- I am a failure.
- I am afraid of _____ and I don't understand why.
- The world is out of control.
- I am alone.
- I am not supported.
- I am out of control.
- I am powerless to make a change in my life.
- I can't be seen and be safe.
- I can't accept responsibility for my actions.
- I can't let others near me.
- I can't make decisions.
- I don't know how to be myself.
- I don't know how to play.
- I don't trust myself.
- I must control my world.
- I must protect myself from others.
- If I let go, I lose control.
- If I make a mistake, I will be hurt.
- It is dangerous to fail.
- It's everyone else's fault.
- Life is a struggle.

- Life is hard.
- Making decisions is dangerous.
- No one is there for me.
- No one listens to me.
- There is only one way to do things: my way, the right way.
- There's no way out.
- What I say is not important.
- You can't trust anyone.
- I am trapped.
- I am guilty of hurting others, and I can't fix what I have done.
- I have no hope for my future.
- What I believed in was all wrong.

Schizophrenia

Schizophrenia is a mental disorder that affects how a person thinks, feels, and behaves. When schizophrenia is active, symptoms can include delusions, hallucinations, disorganized speech, trouble thinking, and lack of motivation.[78] Research has shown that pineal gland calcification may be a factor in the development of schizophrenia.[79]

Repeating Patterns

Missing god's love, feeling unloved, feeling unsafe, disconnected, not knowing what is true, feeling unaccepted, wanting to avoid people, and creating a fantasy for protection.

Emotional States

- ❖ Heavy duty fantasies; the fantasies become the world of reasoning and the thinking adjusts to make the world fit with the fantasies.

- ❖ Fantasy created to explain a fear or trauma-based event that perpetuates the fear (possibly as a child). The fantasy creates the world the way they want.

- ❖ Ego gains power when the fantasies are challenged and the person clings to them even more strongly. (Clarification: Ego would be their identity and the identity built around their perceived reality, fantasies, becomes dominate when others challenge, question, their perceptions. The challenge to their imagination comes from those around them. The more they are challenged, the more their imagination, fantasies, strengthens their identity.)

---

[78] Staff, and reviewed by Felix Torres, M.D., MBA, DFAPA (2020). What is Schizophrenia? American Psychiatric Association. Available from https://www.psychiatry.org/patients-families/schizophrenia/what-is-schizophrenia

[79] Bersani, G., Garavini, A., Taddei, I., Tanfani, G., Nordio, M., & Pancheri, P. (1999). Computed Tomography Study of Pineal Calcification in Schizophrenia. *European Psychiatry, 14(3), 163-166.* Available from https://pubmed.ncbi.nlm.nih.gov/10572342/

- ❖ Reasoning is aligned with fantasies. The reasoning becomes its own reality.

Fears

- ✦ Fear of having no hope
- ✦ Fear of the darkness
- ✦ Fear of the demons
- ✦ Fear of someone trying to kill them
- ✦ Fear that they were guilty of the bad things done to them
- ✦ Fear of being punished by god

Created Patterns

- I can't trust anyone.
- They are all lying to me.
- People hurt me.
- Love is pain.
- God didn't protect me, so I must protect myself.
- I must be important to be loved.
- I must be special to be loved.
- I'm not safe.
- I am disconnected from god.
- God hates me and wants to punish me.
- I'm not loved.
- No one understands me.
- I'm not accepted.

Stroke

A stroke occurs when the blood supply to part of the brain is interrupted or stopped. A blocked blood flow can cause brain cells to die, leading to various symptoms depending on the area of the brain affected.[80] Research has shown a correlation between strokes and pineal gland calcification.[81]

Repeating Patterns

Flow of giving and receiving is blocked. No self-love. No self-care. Can't let go of past hurts. Hold anger around those hurts.

Emotional States

- ❖ Lack of self-confidence in being able to love themselves. Love is stopped. Feels irritable with all around them. Wanting to let go of the feeling of injustice but feel like if they do, they will betray that part of their life. Living in the past. They have not grown with life experiences. There has been a sense of overwhelm, and they stop — can't deal with it anymore.

Fears

- ✦ Fear of having a lack of value
- ✦ Fear of love
- ✦ Fear of overwhelm
- ✦ Fear of living/life
- ✦ Fear of failing
- ✦ Fear of learning

---

[80] National Heart, Lung and Blood Institute(n.d.) What is a stroke? Available from https://www.nhlbi.nih.gov/health/stroke

[81] Kitkhuandee, A., Sawanyawisuth, K., Johns, N. P., Kanpittaya, J., & Johns, J. (2014). Pineal Calcification is Associated with Symptomatic Cerebral Infarction. *Journal of Stroke and Cerebrovascular Diseases: the Official Journal of National Stroke Association*, 23(2), 249–253. Available from https://doi.org/10.1016/j.jstrokecerebrovasdis.2013.01.009

✦ Fear of evolving

Created Patterns

- I feel like giving up.
- I am overloaded and overwhelmed by _____.
- I am being punished for _____.
- I have no patience with myself.
- I can't make myself better.
- I want to die.
- There is no reason to live.
- Life is just too hard to continue.
- I don't love myself; I will never love myself. What's to love?
- I am a failure.
- I am overwhelmed by all of the stuff going wrong. I need to escape.
- I know all there is to know – there's nothing left to learn.

Sexual dysfunction (as it pertains to the pineal gland)

There is some evidence that pineal gland dysfunction may be linked to sexual dysfunction. For example, people with low melatonin levels have been shown to have lower sex drives and sexual function. Additionally, people with certain sleep disorders, such as insomnia, are more likely to experience sexual dysfunction.[82]

Repeating Patterns

- ❖ Doesn't trust others. Resists change. Easily gets into arguments with close relationships. Carries a hidden shame and guilt. Creativity is a lot of starting and stopping and not finishing.

Emotional States

- ❖ Hostile intentions led to a new level of awareness. Awareness that there was a gap in their ability to know right from wrong. The world wasn't what they thought it was. The betrayal left them on guard and vulnerable.

- ❖ Lightning struck (metaphor) – a sudden shock. Their new life was hopeless and meaningless. Silent, knowing that they would never be the same, left them feeling stuck and lost.

- ❖ Shortsighted statements were intended to help, yet they did lots of harm. When they discovered the harm, they took on guilt and shame. They did not feel they could "unring the bell."

---

[82] Bozkurt, A., Karabakan, M., Aktas, B. K., Gunay, M., Keskin, E., & Hirik, E. (2018). Low Serum Melatonin Levels are Associated with Erectile Dysfunction. *International Braz J Urol: Official Journal of the Brazilian Society of Urology, 44(4)*, 794–799. Available from https://doi.org/10.1590/S1677-5538.IBJU.2017.0663

Fears

- ✦ Fears decisions
- ✦ Fears not knowing the answers
- ✦ Fears not knowing the right answer
- ✦ Fears being wrong
- ✦ Fears being lied to
- ✦ Fears being misled
- ✦ Fears trusting others
- ✦ Fears being vulnerable.
- ✦ Fears loss
- ✦ Fears being stuck
- ✦ Fears being alone
- ✦ Fears sudden change
- ✦ Fears being guilty
- ✦ Fears being shamed
- ✦ Fears not being able to fix things
- ✦ Fears loss of power
- ✦ Fears loss of control

Created Patterns

- If I make a decision, I will be shamed.
- If I make a decision, I will be wrong.
- I am always wrong and I am shamed for it.
- If I say something wrong, I can't fix it.
- I am shamed.
- I am guilty of _____.
- Sudden changes are dangerous.
- I can't make a good decision when things change.
- I need to know what to rely upon.
- I am alone.
- When things change, they can't be controlled.
- I must remain in control.
- Change means loss.
- I am alone.
- I am stuck when things change.
- I freeze when asked a question.

- Responsibility is dangerous.
- Responsibility is a burden.
- I second-guess myself.
- I am constantly saying the wrong thing that people won't forgive me for.
- I have lost everything.
- If I am vulnerable, I will be hurt.
- I don't trust people.
- People mislead me.
- People take advantage of me.
- If I am wrong, I will be guilty.
- If I am wrong, I will be shamed.

Appendix D: Physiology and Emotional Pathophysiology of the Pineal Gland

In this chapter, the emotional pathophysiology of pineal gland functions is explored. Emotional pathophysiology is a precursor to an out-of-balance state that will crystallize into a disease and affect intuition. A function that has become out of balance has been affected by specific fears, created patterns and emotional states. I call this emotional pathophysiology. The emotional patterns given in this chapter may become aspects of a disease or be part of an opportunity for a disease to develop.

Melatonin produced by the pineal gland has several functions. Since the pineal gland's primary function is melatonin production, melatonin is the active agent in these functions.

The list of functions is not exhaustive. According to researchers, the pineal gland is still a bit of a mystery. The researchers are still making discoveries. It appears that many research studies are ongoing.

Function: Regulates the Circadian Rhythm and Sleep Cycles

Melatonin is a hormone that plays an essential role in regulating sleep cycles. It helps to signal to the body that it is time to sleep, and it also promotes sleep by increasing the production of sleep-promoting neurotransmitters and decreasing the production of wake-promoting neurotransmitters.

The pineal gland regulates the circadian rhythms and sleep cycles. A light or dark signal from the retina travels via a pathway to the hypothalamus. If the signal is triggered by light, a neuroinhibitor that will block a chemical message is released, and melatonin production is prevented. Alternatively, a neurotransmitter will be triggered by darkness, a chemical message will be released, and the pineal gland will produce melatonin.[83]

Emotional Pathophysiology: Dysregulated Circadian Rhythm and Sleep Cycles Related to Low Melatonin

Repeating Patterns

Powerless, no control, weak boundaries, liver problems, addictions, overwhelm, being taken advantage of, out of sync with others, saying the wrong thing at the wrong time, can't be depended on to make things happen. Toxic projections. Worry. Living in the past or the future. Doesn't understand how the world works. Unable to be a witness; can't be an observer – not present.

---

[83] Arendt J, Aulinas A. *Physiology of the Pineal Gland and Melatonin.* [Updated 2022 Oct 30]. In: Feingold KR, Anawalt B, Blackman MR, et al., editors. Endotext [Internet]. South Dartmouth (MA): MDText.com, Inc.; 2000-. Available from https://www.ncbi.nlm.nih.gov/books/NBK550972/

Emotional States

- Messed-up ideas of right and wrong were forced on them in childhood. Falsehoods were presented as truth and truths were twisted to be what authority (parents, teachers, religious leaders, elders, etc.) wanted them to be. Not knowing what was right or wrong created a push-pull fear of doing the wrong thing. If they stepped forward or tried being responsible, they were subject to ridicule and abuse. These conflicting messages gave them a faulty foundation. So, to be safe, they hold still and only move when mandatory.

- False impression of life. Harsh judgments by others. Judgments for which they were not responsible, but they took them in and felt guilty anyway—carrying the burden of anger and judgments. It was their responsibility to make things nice, to make harmony in an out-of-control, disharmonious environment.

- Out of sync. No sense of up or down. Lack of flow. They go through life in a state of stunned or asleep to what's happening around them. Life happens to them.

- False beingness. An undeveloped sense of self skews their awareness. Communications that fail miss the mark.

- False hope and ideals (direction values) have created chaos. Relationships fail as ideas and concepts are forced into the relationship. This stems from childhoods with parental guidance being misguided and anchored in reaction and fear.

- Lonely knowing. Isolated. A devastating truth held a family secret. They have chosen to be the sacrifice in their knowing.

- Unviable. The life they are living will bring a quick end to their being—a disharmony with the body and its rhythms. Always trying to thwart their nature. A need to escape their body (early life or childhood trauma made being in their body something to escape).

- Shortened cycle of sleep needed to survive. Sleep was never safe. Could be attacked in the night—domestic violence as a child. Always on guard to protect oneself.

- ❖ Doesn't have a sense of knowing what to rely on. Their foundations have crumbled. There is no sense of self-confidence in their abilities, so they must rely on those that will hurt them.

Fears

- ✦ Fear that they will miss out
- ✦ Fear of being attacked
- ✦ Fear of listening to their inner voice
- ✦ Fear of performing to the expectations of others
- ✦ Fear of finding what they are looking for
- ✦ Fear of living
- ✦ Fear of letting others in
- ✦ Fear of being aware of who they are
- ✦ Fear of letting others see who they are
- ✦ Fear of rejection
- ✦ Fear of being known
- ✦ Fear of being vulnerable
- ✦ Fear of being listened to
- ✦ Fear of being responsible
- ✦ Fear of being seen
- ✦ Fear of saying the wrong thing
- ✦ Fear of being bullied
- ✦ Fear of being wrong
- ✦ Fear of being seen as different
- ✦ Fear of change
- ✦ Fear of being judged
- ✦ Fear of being in control

Created Patterns

- I always miss out on the good stuff.
- Sleep is dangerous.
- I will be attacked if I sleep.
- I get lost easily.
- Stuff happens to me.
- If I am heard, I will be hurt.
- No one listens to me.

- I can't let people see who I am; they will hurt me.
- I can't let people see who I am; they will take advantage of me.
- I can't let people see who I am; they will take things from me.
- When people get to know me, they leave.
- I am unloved/unwanted/ rejected.
- I must keep to myself to be safe.
- I can't meet the expectations of others.
- I always disappoint people.
- I am a disappointment.
- I must never stop looking. Otherwise, I will have to stop and take responsibility.
- I never get what I want.
- If I live, I hurt.
- If I live, I lose.
- If I live, I fail.
- If I never connect with others, I will be safe.
- If I never connect with others, I won't be disappointed.
- I will be hurt if I am responsible.
- Being responsible is dangerous.
- I must be invisible.
- If I am seen, I will be hurt.
- If I do anything, I am wrong.
- I am judged.
- I must keep the peace to be safe.
- If I am seen, I will be blamed.
- If I am seen, I will be made responsible.
- I'm always wrong.
- I seem to say the wrong thing at the wrong time.
- Others bully me.
- People ridicule me for my confusion.
- I must pretend to be like everyone else.
- I must blend in to be safe.
- Change is dangerous.
- I am judged when I say the wrong thing.

Function: Strengthens the Immune System

Melatonin has several effects on the immune system, including:[84,85]

- Increase the production of white blood cells, which can help the body fight off infection.
- Activate cytokines, chemical messengers, which can help the body fight off cancer and infection.
- Anti-inflammatory properties can help reduce chronic inflammation and strengthen the immune system.

Emotional Pathophysiology: A Weakened Immune System Related to Low Melatonin

Repeating Patterns

Weak boundaries; people pleasing. Weak response to aggression. Allows self to be overrun. Lack of self-love. Tears self down. Feels a lack of control—a disregard for the boundaries of others.

Emotional States

- ❖ False hopes and false ideas. They realize all their hopes and ideas are false. This led to being fearful of being. They have been in an existential crisis of awareness, not trusting what they see, who they know, and what they feel.

---

[84] Srinivasan V, Maestroni GJ, Cardinali DP, Esquifino AI, Perumal SR, Miller SC. Melatonin, Immune Function and Aging. *Immunity & Ageing*. 2005 Nov 29;2:17. doi: 10.1186/1742-4933-2-17. PMID: 16316470; PMCID: PMC1325257. Available from https://www.ncbi.nlm.nih.gov/pmc/articles/PMC1325257/

[85] Carrillo-Vico, A., Lardone, P. J., Alvarez-Sánchez, N., Rodríguez-Rodríguez, A., & Guerrero, J. M. (2013). Melatonin: Buffering the Immune System. *International Journal of Molecular Sciences, 14(4)*, 8638–8683. Available from https://doi.org/10.3390/ijms14048638

- ❖ Wrong ideas have led them in the wrong direction. These wrong directions mimic the wrong ideas of others, people they trusted. Those they trusted led them astray due to their selfish ideas—an act of betrayal where their needs were not considered.

- ❖ Not enough information to go forward or make decisions. There is never enough information. They are unable to move. If they stay still and are not seen, they won't be hurt; they can't defend themselves.

- ❖ Shut down by others, they halt and go into hyper-awareness. Fearful they will be hurt. They are not worthy of having thoughts of value. They are led to believe they have no value.

Fears

- ✦ Fear of the truth
- ✦ Fear of living
- ✦ Fear of allowing flow
- ✦ Fears their awareness
- ✦ Fears their perceptions
- ✦ Fears trusting anyone or anything
- ✦ Fears being betrayed
- ✦ Fears of being lied to
- ✦ Fears of being taken advantage of
- ✦ Fears making a decision
- ✦ Fear of disappointing people
- ✦ Fears peace

Created Patterns

- I must question everything.
- People betray me.
- My needs are never considered.
- I don't get my needs met.
- I get ignored when I ask for anything.
- I can't believe what people tell me.
- I can't trust people to tell me the truth.
- I can't make decisions.

- If I make a decision, I will be hurt.
- I must analyze everything before making a decision.
- If I make the wrong decision, I will be hurt.
- I can't make a decision until I have enough information.
- I can't move unless I know everything.
- I must create rules to stop people from being disappointed with them.
- I am a disappointment.
- I must make people happy.
- I must be on guard to keep people from diminishing me.
- People put me down.
- I am worthless.
- I'm not good enough.
- People see me as something to be used and thrown away.

Function: Crucial for Reducing the Risk of Cancer

Melatonin reduces the risk of cancer:[86,87]

- As an antioxidant, it helps protect cells from damage caused by free radicals. Free radicals are unstable molecules that can damage DNA, leading to cancer.
- It has anti-inflammatory properties, which can help reduce cancer risk.
- Boosts the immune system.
- Promotes apoptosis, a natural process of cell death, in cancer cells, which can help to prevent cancer growth.
- By inhibiting the growth of new blood vessels, it keeps cancer from growing and spreading.

Emotional Pathophysiology: Elevated Risk of Cancer Because of Low Melatonin

Repeating Patterns

Generational hopelessness. The past is eating them up inside, causing self-destruction. What eats them up? What consumes them? Hate? Revenge? Resentment? Guilt? Generational hopelessness.

Emotional States

- ❖ Wasted efforts at stopping angry people from hurting them. Warrantless anger directed at them was a trauma held by the angry people –

---

[86] Davoodvandi, A., Nikfar, B., Reiter, R.J. *et al.* Melatonin and Cancer Suppression: Insights into its Effects on DNA Methylation. *Cell Mol Biol Lett* **27**, 73 (2022). Available from https://doi.org/10.1186/s11658-022-00375-z

[87] Li, Y., Li, S., Zhou, Y., Meng, X., Zhang, J. J., Xu, D. P., & Li, H. B. (2017). Melatonin for the Prevention and Treatment of Cancer. *Oncotarget*, *8*(24), 39896–39921. Available from https://doi.org/10.18632/oncotarget.16379.

they needed to make other people hurt because they hurt. (ancestral, epigenetic, or early childhood)

- ❖ Short-term awareness brought angst and anger. Led to believe they were in control, and then they were betrayed and misled. Finally, they became powerless with a feeling of no choice.

- ❖ Walled off feelings about a mystery that was built around a family secret. A sense of lost hope was the thread that wound its way through the family.

- ❖ False ideas about life led them to abandon their hopes and dreams. They have led a life of drudgery and despair. No sense that there is any hope that life will get any better.

- ❖ Major differences between themselves and their ancestry have created a hate-filled division. This ancestral division did not foster peace; instead created angst and reactive motives for undermining their life.

Fears

- ✦ Fear of angry people
- ✦ Fear of being unjustly accused
- ✦ Fear of being out of control
- ✦ Fear of being powerless
- ✦ Fear of being betrayed
- ✦ Fear of being trapped
- ✦ Fear of having no choice
- ✦ Fear of being found
- ✦ Fear of the family secrets being found out
- ✦ Fear of living
- ✦ Fear of challenging the status quo
- ✦ Fear of disappearing
- ✦ Fear of the family
- ✦ Fear of nothingness
- ✦ Fear of being alone
- ✦ Fear of what others think

Created Patterns

- I am the whipping boy.
- I always get blamed for everything.
- I can't stop people from hurting me.
- I have no choices.
- People betray me.
- I get blamed for everything.
- I am powerless in the face of others' anger.
- I have no hope.
- I can't allow myself to feel.
- I have no dreams.
- I must hide from angry people.
- I must get away from angry people.
- Life is drudgery.
- Life will never be better.
- I am a victim.
- Bad things always happen to me.
- The old ways are hypocrisy.
- The "way it's always been" hurts people who are different.
- Angry people are dangerous.
- I am unjustly accused.
- I am nobody.

Function: Melatonin Increases Bone Regeneration

Melatonin has been shown to have several effects on bone health, including:[88]

- Increase the production of cells that build new bone.
- Decrease the production of cells that break down bone.
- Increase the absorption of calcium from the gut.
- Decrease the excretion of calcium in the urine.

Emotional Pathophysiology: Decreased Bone Regeneration Because of Low Melatonin

Repeating Patterns

Resentment that has removed their integrity. Hardened feelings of anger and injustice. There is a bitterness tearing down or eroding structure.

Emotional States

- ❖ False hopes and ideals came crashing down. Left them bereft with no concept of who they were. Identity was shattered—lost everything. Not allowing themselves to evolve; instead, they continue to resurrect the old identity. The old identity gives them some sense of where to go, but it continues to collapse. They feel lost.

- ❖ Harsh realities and a harsh life brought them depression and despair. Short – they are short in stature. No sense that they can change or travel out of the land they live in.

---

[88] Liu, J., Huang, F., & He, H.-W. (2013). Melatonin Effects on Hard Tissues: Bone and Tooth. *International Journal of Molecular Sciences*, *14*(5), 10063–10074. Available from https://doi.org/10.3390/ijms140510063

- ❖ Narrow focus and narrow hopes shut the doors. Fears of opening to new ideas or ways of thinking. Their structured life is not as safe as they think. Whining got them less support and more alienation.

- ❖ Harsh lessons were unrelenting. Trust failed. Friends failed; what they had depended on collapsed. All taking and no giving. Must keep giving to be wanted and loved.

- ❖ Heritage subjected them to a feeling of being beaten down by animosity. They crumpled under the weight. [89]

- ❖ What they depended on in a love or intimate relationship was not what they had anticipated. Leaving them with an unanswered need to feel supported and cared for.

Fears

- ✦ Fear of being unloved/unwanted
- ✦ Fear of being unsupported
- ✦ Fear of abandonment
- ✦ Fear of being alone
- ✦ Fear of change
- ✦ Fear of letting go of the old ways
- ✦ Fear that nothing will ever be better
- ✦ Fear of being trapped
- ✦ Fear of being less than
- ✦ Fear of pushing back
- ✦ Fear of standing up
- ✦ Fear of trusting others
- ✦ Fear of being reliant on others
- ✦ Fear of losing everything
- ✦ Fear of having everything taken from them
- ✦ Fear of being forced against their will

---

[89] Chen P, Li Z, Hu Y. Prevalence of Osteoporosis in China: a Meta-Analysis and Systematic Review. *BMC Public Health*. 2016 Oct 3;16(1):1039. Available from https://link.springer.com/article/10.1186/s12889-016-3712-7. PMID: 27716144; PMCID: PMC5048652.

✦ Fear of being crushed

Created Patterns

- Everything about me is false.
- I am living a lie.
- I am trapped in my life.
- I have no options for improving my lot in life.
- Life is hard.
- I can't depend on others.
- I am unloved/unwanted.
- I am alone.
- New ideas are dangerous.
- New ideas will cause chaos.
- New ideas cause pain.
- I must work hard to stay safe and alive.
- If I don't obey, I will be destroyed.
- I have no identity.
- I have no purpose.
- I must hide to stay safe.
- I can't be seen and be safe.
- I must be small to be unseen and stay safe.
- My life is a prison, and there is no escape.
- I'm not worthy of a life.
- If I stand up, I will be hurt/killed.
- I have no dreams or hopes.
- No one helps me.
- I am unsupported.

Function: Protecting Against Oxidative Stress

Oxidative stress is a condition that occurs when there is an imbalance between the production of free radicals and the body's ability to neutralize them. Free radicals are unstable molecules that can damage cells and tissues produced in oxygen metabolization. Antioxidants are molecules that can help neutralize free radicals.[90] Unfortunately, the repair process is overwhelmed if too many free radicals exist. Oxidative stress is one of the known factors in cognitive aging[91], cancer, diabetes, atherosclerosis, inflammation, hypertension, heart disease, and neurodegenerative diseases such as Parkinson's and Alzheimer's. Melatonin is an antioxidant that can help protect against the damage caused by oxidative stress by reducing toxic free radicals.[92,93]

Emotional Pathophysiology: Impaired Protection Against Oxidative Stress Because of Low Melatonin

Repeating Patterns

Overwhelm. Being taken over. Freewill hijacked. Self-destruction when overwhelmed. Too much ___(fill in the blank)_____ becomes bad. Difficult relationship with the feminine (mother).

---

[90] Megan Dix, RN, BSN (2018). Everything You Would Know About Oxidative Stress. *Healthline*. Available from https://www.healthline.com/health/oxidative-stress

[91] Ionescu-Tucker, A., & Cotman, C. W. (2021). Emerging Roles of Oxidative Stress in Brain Aging and Alzheimer's Disease. *Neurobiology of Aging, 107, 86–95*. Available from https://doi.org/10.1016/j.neurobiolaging.2021.07.014

[92] Mojgan Morvaridzadeh, Ehsan Sadeghi, Shahram Agah, Seyed Mostafa Nachvak, Siavash Fazelian, Fatemeh Moradi, Emma Persad, Javad Heshmati (2020). Effect of Elatonin Supplementation on Oxidative Stress Parameters: A Systematic Review and Meta-Analysis. *Pharmacological Research, Volume 161*, 2020,105210, ISSN 1043-6618. Available from https://doi.org/10.1016/j.phrs.2020.105210

[93] Reiter, R.J., Mayo, J.C., Tan, D.-X., Sainz, R.M., Alatorre-Jimenez, M. and Qin, L. (2016). Melatonin as an Antioxidant: Under Promises but over Delivers. *J. Pineal Res.*, 61: 253-278. Available from https://doi.org/10.1111/jpi.12360

Emotional States

- Shortfall of energy and passion to do anything. Lost their will and have a feeling of no purpose. Shut out of their need to hold on to life's pleasure. They retreat, pull back and don't seek what they don't have. They give up on passion and purpose.

- Wired differently than others, they yield to the winds of change, and then they don't flow with the change. Shortsighted, they do not give themselves the ability to engage; instead, they hide in the change without the change.

- Junt* (costly items, gaudy) is focused on the external. Junt becomes the identity. Focus on external physical adornment and physical pleasure—acceptance and identity based on junt.

    Junt has multiple meanings in urban slang. The meaning used here refers to large, costly items, gaudy.
    https://www.urbandictionary.com/define.php?term=junt

- Wiped out, then rises again to be wiped out again. Shelves attempt to rise and stays flat out. Energy for moving through life has evaporated. There's no motivation, no purpose.

Fears

- Fear of love
- Fear of being unloved
- Fear of being unwanted
- Fear of my anger
- Fear they can't live up to expectations
- Fear of flow
- Fear of living
- Fear of peace
- Fear of being powerless
- Fear of change
- Fear of being different
- Fear of the shadow
- Fear of self
- Fear of knowing

- ✦ Fear of success
- ✦ Fear of being known
- ✦ Fear of the mother
- ✦ Fear of the divine feminine

Created Patterns

- I am unloved.
- I am unwanted.
- I am overwhelmed.
- When I am overwhelmed, I hurt myself.
- I am bitter toward _____.
- I hate _____.
- I can't do anything right.
- I am always wrong.
- I can't make a difference, so why even try?
- No matter how hard I try, I can never get ahead.
- I must stay in control, or I will be hurt.
- I have no control over anything I do.
- My mother does not want me.
- My mother does not love me.
- I am uncared for.
- Life is dangerous.
- Living is dangerous and hard.
- I can't have peace.
- I am never happy.
- I am never satisfied.
- I can't find happiness.
- I must stay invisible.
- I will never get what I want in life.
- I am unsuccessful.
- The good stuff is for others, not me.
- Change is dangerous.
- I must hide from people.

Function: Improves Neurogenesis and Synaptic Plasticity

Studies have shown that melatonin is cardinal (very important) to promoting neurogenesis and synaptic plasticity. Synaptic plasticity is our brain's ability to adjust to new information. Neurogenesis is the continual creation of nerve tissue. Neurogenesis and synaptic plasticity allow our brains to learn and create memories.[94]

Emotional Pathophysiology: Impaired Neurogenesis and Synaptic Plasticity Because of Low Melatonin.

Repeating Patterns

Not being able to adjust to change. Can't incorporate new information, a trauma that stops memory(ies). Overwhelming trauma, such as PTSD, ACOA, violence, and loss. Stuck in grief. Flow is stopped. Stuck in time.

Emotional States

- ❖ Hopeless, don't feel their life will get any better. They are stuck in their doom and gloom (ancestral/epigenetic). A way of protecting themselves. A hostile history of having the good things taken away, so that is how they live their lives.

- ❖ Everything stopped. Life stopped, and reason stopped. They stopped breathing – held their breath. They have no ability to know why or how their life had been taken. They stopped all movement and froze. No one came. No one was interested in helping when a devastating tragedy struck.

---

[94] Song, J. Pineal Gland Dysfunction in Alzheimer's Disease: Relationship with the Immune-Pineal Axis, Sleep Disturbance, and Neurogenesis. *Mol Neurodegeneration* 14, 28 (2019). Available from https://doi.org/10.1186/s13024-019-0330-8

- ❖ They hung onto the muck. Their thinking became clogged with all the residue of secrets. They felt guilt and blame. They felt as if they would not tell others and reach a place of peace.

- ❖ Low-energy and low-vibration people dominated their life and told them what to think and what to do. They gave over their agency to keep the peace. They kept quiet and allowed their life to be absorbed.

- ❖ They are unconnected. Messages (communication) are not heard. They speak and no one hears them. They are invisible and silent. Hostile energies want them shut down and shut up. They want them silenced so they will not get resources.

Fears

- ✦ Fear of the future
- ✦ Fears of having good things
- ✦ Fears people will take from them
- ✦ Fears being happy
- ✦ Fear of breathing
- ✦ Fear of life
- ✦ Fear of someone learning the secrets
- ✦ Fear of letting go
- ✦ Fear of freedom
- ✦ Fear of making decisions
- ✦ Fear of being heard
- ✦ Fear of being
- ✦ Fear of being seen
- ✦ Fear of having a better life
- ✦ Fear of standing up
- ✦ Fear of good things happening
- ✦ Fear of change
- ✦ Fear of remembering
- ✦ Fear of flow
- ✦ Fear of being out of control
- ✦ Fear of chaos

Created Patterns

- I'm not good enough.
- I am worthless.
- I'm not worthy.
- No one wants to know I exist.
- Good things are taken from me.
- I can't have good things.
- Everything is hopeless.
- Change is dangerous.
- I must keep things the same to be safe.
- I must be in control to be safe.
- People take my good things.
- Good things are taken away from me.
- If I am seen, I will be hurt.
- If I stand up for myself, I am assaulted.
- If my life is better than others (family, friends), I will be hurt.
- My family takes things from me.
- If I speak up, I will be blamed.
- If I make a decision, I get blamed for being wrong, even if it was a good decision.
- I can't do anything right.
- I can't let go.
- I must keep the secrets at all costs.
- I can't breathe easily; I must be on guard all the time.
- If someone hears me breathing, I will be hurt.
- When I am happy, someone always takes it away.
- I am hopeless.
- My life will never be good.
- I am guilty of _____.
- I will never have peace.
- I must put up with mean people to keep the peace.
- No one hears me.

Function: Suppressing Neuroinflammation

Neuroinflammation is a condition that occurs when the immune system becomes activated in the brain. This condition can damage brain cells and tissues and contribute to neurological disorders such as Alzheimer's disease, Parkinson's disease, and multiple sclerosis.[95,96,97]

Melatonin suppresses neuroinflammation by:

- **Reducing the production of pro-inflammatory cytokines**. Cytokines are proteins that act as signaling molecules between cells. Cytokines tell the cells they need to mount an offense and increase the production of anti-inflammatory cytokines (Cytokines are small proteins that play a crucial role in cell signaling and communication within the immune system). Research has shown melatonin suppresses the release of proinflammatory cytokines.

- **Inhibit the activation of microglia, which are the brain's immune cells**. When microglia become activated, they release several chemicals that can damage brain cells and tissues. Melatonin can help to prevent microglia from becoming activated and releasing these chemicals. Melatonin is an immune modulator that balances the immune and inflammatory responses.

- **Protecting brain cells from damage by free radicals**. Free radicals are unstable molecules that can damage cells and tissues. Melatonin can help to neutralize free radicals and protect brain cells from damage.

---

[95] Won, E., Na, K. S., & Kim, Y. K. (2021). Associations between Melatonin, Neuroinflammation, and Brain Alterations in Depression. *International Journal of Molecular Sciences, 23(1), 305.* Available from https://doi.org/10.3390/ijms23010305

[96] Hardeland R. (2019). Aging, Melatonin, and the Pro- and Anti-Inflammatory Networks. *International Journal of Molecular Sciences, 20(5), 1223.* Available from https://doi.org/10.3390/ijms20051223

[97] Hardeland R. Melatonin and inflammation—Story of a double-edged blade. *J. Pineal Res. 2018;* 65:e12525. Available from https://doi.org/10.1111/jpi.12525

Emotional Pathophysiology: Impaired Neuroinflammation Suppression Because of Low Melatonin

Repeating Patterns

Anger, hatred, irritation, aggression, impatience, impulsive behavior, stress, and anxiety. No peace, feeling violated, reactive response for protection. ACOA, C-PTSD, PTSD, Sexual Abuse, Domestic Violence, childhood violence. Feels under assault.

Emotional States

- ❖ Poor choices in life left them hurt and afraid. They did not know how to stop the flow of abuse. They could not stop people from hurting them and still make people happy. Poor boundaries.

- ❖ Warnings of impending doom went unheard. They did not plan. They did not look for solutions. They ignored those who tried to prepare them. They went into denial that this was happening. They refused to change their course.

Fears

- ✦ Fear of hearing bad things
- ✦ Fear of having to deal with a difficult reality
- ✦ Fear of making decisions
- ✦ Fear of being told they are wrong
- ✦ Fear of being overrun
- ✦ Fear of being ignored
- ✦ Fear of being disrespected
- ✦ Fear of being dismissed
- ✦ Fear of being taken advantage of
- ✦ Fear of being out of control
- ✦ Fear of being trapped
- ✦ Fear of losing freedom
- ✦ Fear of being hurt
- ✦ Fear of overwhelm

✦ Fear of being punished

Created Patterns

- I have to run away to be safe.
- I am nothing.
- When I get yelled at, I shut down and get overwhelmed.
- I am not good enough.
- I am ignored.
- I must let people hurt me to make them happy.
- I must let people hurt me to have peace.
- I am trapped.
- People blame me for being bad and then hurt me.
- I get blamed for nothing I did.
- I can't stop people from hurting me.
- I can't get out of the abuse.
- I have no support.
- I am unloved/unwanted/uncared for.
- I make bad choices.
- When I do something wrong, then they pay attention to me.
- Being hurt is how I survive.
- I am angry at _____.
- I hate _____.

Function: Modulates the Immune Response

If the body's immune response overreacts, melatonin will tamp down the response. If the body's response is impaired, melatonin will enhance the immune response. Melatonin can activate or suppress immune cells.[98]

Emotional Pathophysiology: Unmodulated Immune Response Because of Low Melatonin

Repeating Patterns

Never know how to react, and every reaction is incorrect; too much or too little. Doesn't show up when needed. Weak boundaries or over strong boundaries, both being inappropriate reactions in the situation where they are invoked. Needs to remain in control.

Emotional States

- ❖ Wrong information conveyed to them. They reacted with vim and vigor to the wrong information – pushing against the wrong thing—anger at being made to look stupid by someone who gave them the wrong information.

- ❖ Nervous focus led them into a path of high anxiety. Pushing back against the path, their reaction fueled the anxiety and became an overwhelming attack on those they thought were responsible. They held a hyper-vigilant state so that they wouldn't be wrong, and still, it happened.

---

[98] Carrillo-Vico, A., Lardone, P. J., Alvarez-Sánchez, N., Rodríguez-Rodríguez, A., & Guerrero, J. M. (2013). Melatonin: Buffering the Immune System. *International Journal of Molecular Sciences, 14(4)*, 8638–8683. Available from https://doi.org/10.3390/ijms14048638

- ❖ Wrath at being invaded/boundaries overrun by those that felt they could take what they wanted. Huge overreaction. They went from powerless to powerful with no control. They just knew they needed to stop them.

- ❖ Feeling blamed and resentful, they lash out at those that want to take what they have. The others felt they had that right. Familial/ancestral/epigenetic.

Fears

- ✦ Fear of no control
- ✦ Fear of being wrong
- ✦ Fears being depended on
- ✦ Fears being where they have no control
- ✦ Fears being seen as stupid
- ✦ Fears being untrustworthy
- ✦ Fears being led astray
- ✦ Fear of being overrun
- ✦ Fear of their power
- ✦ Fear of having their things taken
- ✦ Fears being blamed
- ✦ Fear of family
- ✦ Fears being taken advantage of

Created Patterns

- I'm not good enough.
- People take advantage of me.
- I have no control.
- If I am wrong, I will be punished.
- Others try to make me look stupid.
- I am stupid.
- My family is out of control.
- I can't protect myself from my family.
- I am overrun.
- People take advantage of me.
- People take things from me.

- People lie to me.
- I am unjustly accused.
- I get blamed for stuff I didn't do.
- I don't take responsibility.
- I let other people tell me what to do so I am not blamed.
- My family betrayed me.
- I am abandoned / alone.
- I overreact to get people to listen.

Function: Enhancing Memory Function

Melatonin enhances memory function by:[99,100]

- Promoting neurogenesis, which is the growth of new brain cells. New brain cells are essential for learning and memory.

- Helping to strengthen memories by promoting the consolidation of memories into long-term storage.

- Helping to protect against memory loss by reducing the damage caused by free radicals and other toxins.

Emotional Pathophysiology: Impaired Memory Function Because of Low Melatonin

Repeating Patterns

They do not think others are interested in what they know, so they think it's no use remembering what they know.

Emotional States

- ❖ False impressions were used to replace images that have disappeared – the impressions are disconnected in the timeline, so they just float. Feeling small and irrelevant wants to be invisible and disappear. They have nothing of value to offer the world. They are nothing, moving to nothingness.

---

[99] Hikaru Iwashita, Yukihisa Matsumoto, Yusuke Maruyama, Kazuki Watanabe, Atsuhiko Chiba, Atsuhiko Hattori (2020). The Melatonin Metabolite N1-acetyl-5-methoxykynuramine Facilitates Long-Term Object Memory in Young and Aging Mice. *Journal of Pineal Research Vol 70 Issue 1*. Available from https://doi.org/10.1111/jpi.12703

[100] Zakaria, R., Ahmad, A. H., & Othman, Z. (2016). The Potential Role of Melatonin on Memory Function: Lessons from Rodent Studies. *Folia Biologica*, 62(5), 181–187. Available from https://fb.cuni.cz/file/5818/fb2016a0022.pdf

- ❖ Lack of presence in the moment when a memory was experienced – lights were on, but they weren't home. They are just going through the motions.

- ❖ A trauma so great that they do not have the emotional skills or strength to handle what they have experienced. They then shut the memory down. If remembering means many years of trauma, then whole lifetimes or blocks of time may be erased.

- ❖ No hope. Doesn't feel they can change things. Life is hard and unchanging. Feels they are controlled by a system that is rigged against them. They lack the confidence to make the changes needed to bring sunshine into their lives.

Fears

- ✦ Fear of nothingness
- ✦ Fear of being relegated
- ✦ Fear of isolation
- ✦ Fear of being alone
- ✦ Fear of becoming obsolete
- ✦ Fear of being reduced to irrelevant
- ✦ Fear of being worthless
- ✦ Fear of getting old
- ✦ Fear of dying
- ✦ Fear of being invisible
- ✦ Fear of being present
- ✦ Fear of being in their body
- ✦ Fear of remembering
- ✦ Fear of life
- ✦ Fear of flow
- ✦ Fear of the institutions
- ✦ Fear of being stuck in one place
- ✦ Fear of remembering the pain
- ✦ Fear of authority
- ✦ Fear of being in control

Created Patterns

- I am nothing.
- I am alone.
- I am isolated.
- No one cares what I think.
- I am obsolete.
- I no longer matter.
- I am worthless.
- I'm not good enough.
- I am old and will die soon.
- I am invisible.
- Being present hurts.
- My body fails me.
- If I remember, I will feel guilt/shame/regrets/anger.
- Remembering makes me feel bad.
- Remembering hurts.
- All they want is my money and then to kill me off.
- If you try to live, they will take everything away, so you can't.
- I can't allow them to keep taking from me.
- If they keep taking, then there will be nothing left.
- My life is all wrong.

Function: Plays a Role in Spatial Navigation

Melatonin plays a role in spatial navigation by increasing the number of new neurons generated in the hippocampus. This brain region is essential for spatial navigation.[101]

Emotional Pathophysiology: Impaired Spatial Navigation

Repeating Patterns

A feeling of lost, not knowing what direction to go, not feeling a sense of purpose.

Emotional States

- ❖ Jumbled information that was impossible to sort through created confusion, overwhelm and inner chaos. Destruction of one's sense of identity (as a child) – a parenting process of breaking a child's will. (ancestral/epigenetic)

- ❖ Unwanted. Unwarranted physical abuse (random). Fear of impending violence. Freeze response. Doesn't know what to do to escape.

Fears

- ✦ Fear of being out of control
- ✦ Fear of being lost
- ✦ Fear of having no purpose
- ✦ Fear of being vulnerable
- ✦ Fear of being their true self
- ✦ Fear of violence

---

[101] Bayliss, C. R., Bishop, N. L., & Fowler, R. C. (1985). Pineal Gland Calcification and Defective Sense of Direction. *British Medical Journal (Clinical Research ed.)*, 291(6511), 1758–1759. Available from https://doi.org/10.1136/bmj.291.6511.1758

- ✦ Fear of the unknown
- ✦ Fear of humiliation
- ✦ Fear of being crushed
- ✦ Fear of diminishment
- ✦ Fear of being destroyed
- ✦ Fear of having a presence
- ✦ Fear of being trapped

Created Patterns

- I am lost.
- I have no control.
- I am powerless.
- I don't know where I am going.
- I am trapped.
- I have no purpose.
- There is no escape from a life of hopelessness.
- I can't let people see "me."
- The unknown is dangerous.
- Bad things are going to happen.
- Bad things will happen to me.
- I am unloved/unwanted.
- I am alone.
- There is no escape from my life.
- As long as I am confused, I am safe.
- I go into overwhelm to stay safe.
- I am a nobody.
- I am worthless.
- I have no value.
- No one loves me.
- I get beaten if I'm not good enough.
- I get beaten without a reason.
- I freeze when there is violence.
- I can't save myself.
- I am unwanted.

Function: Controlling the Timing and Release of Female and Male Reproductive Hormones

Melatonin is vital in regulating the timing and release of female and male reproductive hormones. It helps to ensure that these hormones are produced at the right time and in the right amounts, which is essential for fertility.[102,103]

Emotional Pathophysiology: Dysregulated Timing and Release of Female and Male Reproductive Hormones

Repeating Patterns

Control and regulation of creativity, feeling out of control, suppressed imagination, not allowed to play.

Emotional States

- ❖ Wrong direction in life – constantly feels like they are hitting one brick wall after another. They get nowhere. Getting nowhere and accomplishing nothing is a place of safety for them. Trauma created a need to stay invisible; that way, no one wants anything from them. Makes wrong decisions. Stays away from responsibility.

- ❖ Hot mess. Life is a constant struggle with a feeling of discombobulation. Chaos reigns. Abandoned and rejected early in life. Trying to figure out where they belong.

---

[102] Olcese J. M. (2020). Melatonin and Female Reproduction: An Expanding Universe. *Frontiers in Endocrinology*, 11, 85. Available from https://doi.org/10.3389/fendo.2020.00085

[103] Lerchl, A. and Luboshitzky, R. (2004), Melatonin Administration Alters Semen Quality in Normal Men. *Journal of Andrology*, 25: 185-187. Available from https://doi.org/10.1002/j.1939-4640.2004.tb02778.x

- ❖ Short-term anxiety rises up and releases. Safe/unsafe. Trauma of the mind – a relationship with a narcissist that controlled their thoughts. A form of brainwashing left them struggling to make sense of the world.

- ❖ Creation and imagination killed to control them. They were told what to think, what to imagine and how to imagine and create. They became the identity that was defined for them.

Fears

- ✦ Fears of being out of control
- ✦ Fears being seen
- ✦ Fears success
- ✦ Fears being asked to do
- ✦ Fears making decisions
- ✦ Fears responsibility
- ✦ Fears doing anything creative
- ✦ Fears peace
- ✦ Fears being forced against their will
- ✦ Fears being found
- ✦ Fears life
- ✦ Fears life changes
- ✦ Fears being unwanted
- ✦ Fears not belonging
- ✦ Fears making their own decisions
- ✦ Fears rejection
- ✦ Fears being ostracized

Created Patterns

- I am rejected.
- I am ostracized.
- I do not belong.
- I don't know where I belong.
- I can't make decisions.
- Change is dangerous.
- Change causes things to be out of control.

- Change will hurt you.
- I am out of control.
- I must stay in control to be safe.
- If I am seen, I will be hurt.
- If I am seen I will be forced against my will to _____.
- Making decisions will get you judged.
- Making decisions will get you hurt.
- I don't know what peace is.
- I can never have peace.
- Responsibility is rewarded with pain.
- Responsibility will get you hurt.
- I am forced against my will.
- Success is dangerous; people will take it from you.
- If I am found, they will hurt me.
- I do not belong.
- I am unwanted.
- If I do anything creative, I am criticized.
- I must hide my creativity to be safe.

Function: Restores the body

Melatonin is a hormone that has several beneficial effects on the body. It can help to reduce inflammation, boost the immune system, repair cells, promote healing, relieve pain, and improve sleep.[104,105,106,107,108]

Emotional Pathophysiology: Lack of Body Restoration Because of Low Melatonin

Repeating Patterns

Ungrounded. Disconnected from people. Wants to be alone; knows how to survive alone. No sense of purpose. Lost. No foundation. Numb heart. Parental dysfunction. No trust. Frozen in grief. Lung issues. Abused as a child.

---

[104] Srinivasan V, Maestroni GJ, Cardinali DP, Esquifino AI, Perumal SR, Miller SC. Melatonin, Immune Function and Aging. *Immunity & Ageing.* 2005 Nov 29;2:17. doi: 10.1186/1742-4933-2-17. PMID: 16316470; PMCID: PMC1325257. Available from https://www.ncbi.nlm.nih.gov/pmc/articles/PMC1325257/

[105] Reiter, R. J., Calvo, J. R., Karbownik, M., Qi, W., & Tan, D. X. (2000). Melatonin and its Relation to the Immune System and Inflammation. *Annals of the New York Academy of Sciences, 917*, 376–386. Available from https://doi.org/10.1111/j.1749-6632.2000.tb05402.x

[106] Vaseenon, S., Chattipakorn, N., & Chattipakorn, S. C. (2021). Effects of Melatonin in Wound Healing of Dental Pulp and Periodontium: Evidence from In Vitro, In Vivo and Clinical studies. *Archives of Oral Biology, 123*, 105037. Available from https://doi.org/10.1016/j.archoralbio.2020.105037

[107] Xie, S., Fan, W., He, H., & Huang, F. (2020). Role of Melatonin in the Regulation of Pain. *Journal of Pain Research, 13*, 331–343. Available from https://doi.org/10.2147/JPR.S228577

[108] Zisapel N. (2018). New Perspectives on the Role of Melatonin in Human sleep, Circadian Rhythms and their Regulation. *British journal of Pharmacology, 175*(16), 3190–3199. Available from https://doi.org/10.1111/bph.14116

Emotional States

- ❖ A sense of not belonging where they are or even on this planet. They feel uncomfortable in their family and their circle of friends. They feel homeless and untethered. Rejected early in life, they have no attachment or connection for fear it will be taken from them.

- ❖ Aimless pursuit of nothing. A life of dead ends and powerful headwinds caused them to feel lost. They were emotionally abandoned by parents that did not want children. They had no foundation or models of grounded behavior or love.

- ❖ Wanting without fulfillment, they were left in a void of darkness of push-pull with no shore to land on. Empty. Fears someone is trying to connect with them. There was a hatred for those that had untethered their life.

- ❖ Empty heart, a deep sense of emptiness. Nothingness. Risked it all and failed – deep guilt ravaged their being, and to survive, they closed off their heart feelings.

Fears

- ✦ Fears of being close to others
- ✦ Fears family
- ✦ Fears friends
- ✦ Fears their heart
- ✦ Fears connection
- ✦ Fears love
- ✦ Fears anger
- ✦ Fears living
- ✦ Fears of being unable to escape
- ✦ Fears of being trapped in a room of people
- ✦ Fears authenticity
- ✦ Fears trusting anything or anyone

Created Patterns

- I'm unlovable.
- I'm unwanted.
- I'm alone.
- I can't get away from the hatred.
- I must protect myself from people.
- Angry people are dangerous.
- My family is angry and mean.
- I do not trust myself.
- I don't trust people.
- I am safe alone.
- I can't do anything right.
- I must protect my heart from others.
- I can never do anything right.
- I am constantly second-guessing myself.
- I can't tell when people are deceiving me.
- I am always different from others.
- I don't fit in.
- I can't ever get what I want.
- There's no safe place for me.
- Good things do not happen to me.

Function: Regulation of the Pituitary Gland

The pituitary gland is a small gland located at the brain's base. It is responsible for producing several hormones, including growth hormone, thyroid-stimulating hormone, and adrenocorticotropic hormone. Melatonin can help regulate the production of these hormones by increasing the production of growth hormones, thyroid-stimulating hormones, and adrenocorticotropic hormones (a hormone your pituitary gland releases that triggers your adrenal glands to release cortisol, the "stress hormone").[109]

Emotional Pathophysiology: Dysregulated Pituitary Gland Because of Low Melatonin

Repeating Patterns

Thinks people are taking advantage and they feel they have lost control. They must stay in control to feel safe. Alone. May harbor feelings of revenge. Untrusting. Overreaction when boundaries are threatened. Surface only – no depth to interactions. Childhood adults were critical and manipulating with little support or love.

Emotional States

- ❖ Falsehood in their lives led them astray. Caused them to feel obligated to those that lied to them. They were then manipulated and controlled by those liars.

- ❖ Many reasons were given as to why their life was being judged. They disconnected from it all. Even the disconnection was judged. Others

---

[109] Ciani, E., Haug, T. M., Maugars, G., Weltzien, F. A., Falcón, J., & Fontaine, R. (2021). Effects of Melatonin on Anterior Pituitary Plasticity: A Comparison Between Mammals and Teleosts. *Frontiers in Endocrinology*, 11, 605111. Available from https://doi.org/10.3389/fendo.2020.605111

judged them so they would not be different and move outside the judger's control.

- ❖ Retribution was at hand. They had been hurt and sought to get even with their persecutors. They lived for justice and a balancing payback.

- ❖ Wild thoughts and irrational emotions destroyed their peace. They felt others were out to take advantage and hurt them. They had lost trust in all the people that supposedly tried to help them and only ended up hurting them.

- ❖ Shift in ideologies was narrowly seen. (Clarification: This is a refusal to change. New concepts or ideas create a shutting down.) No depth of understanding. Tunnel vision. Locked their world into the limited experience of relationships where there was an exchange. Nothing was safe; they had to keep everything under control, and they could only control a small amount. Ancestral/familial/epigenetic.

- ❖ Meaningless chatter dominated their lives. They refused to be seen as vulnerable or give people any real idea of who they are. Deeply wounded by bullies in school and home, their identities were attacked. Vowed to hide their identity so they would not be dissed.

- ❖ Withering looks destroyed their sense of well-being and self-confidence. They knew they were less than others and were destroyed inside.

- ❖ Wound up tightly, they weren't aware of the world. They couldn't see it or their relationships due to their winding. All they could see was their own stuff. If they saw outside of themselves, they would be unsafe and hurt.

- ❖ Wanton disregard for others as they focus on themselves only. The disregard meant me-first selfish. Pulled inside -- only for them; narcissistic. Familial survival.

Fears

- ✦ Fears trusting others
- ✦ Fears putting themselves out
- ✦ Fears flow
- ✦ Fears connection
- ✦ Fears being seen
- ✦ Fears attack
- ✦ Fears being vulnerable
- ✦ Fears change
- ✦ Fears new information
- ✦ Fears being taken advantage of
- ✦ Fears of being out of control
- ✦ Fears of being ripped off
- ✦ Fears injustice
- ✦ Fears being controlled
- ✦ Fears being judged
- ✦ Fears being manipulated
- ✦ Fears being obligated
- ✦ Fears being lied to
- ✦ Fears love

Created Patterns

- I am judged.
- I must protect myself from people who want to manipulate and take from me.
- I want revenge against _____.
- When I am vulnerable, I am hurt.
- I am lied to and manipulated by others.
- Obligation is a trap.
- I am abused.
- People want me only for what I can do for them.
- I am unsupported.
- I am unloved.
- I can't trust people not to hurt me.
- People can't be trusted.
- I don't trust myself.
- The people that should love me lie to me.

- People only want me around for what I can do for them.
- I must be in control to be safe.
- People try to manipulate me.
- People are always trying to rip me off.
- People take advantage of me.
- If I am not in control, I will be hurt.
- Change is dangerous.
- New information is dangerous.
- I am under attack.
- I am unsupported.
- I am alone.
- I need to push others away to be safe.
- I don't love

Function: Glucose Homeostasis and Energy Balance

Melatonin helps improve insulin sensitivity, meaning cells can use glucose for energy. This function can help to lower blood sugar levels. Melatonin also helps to reduce the production of glucose by the liver. This reduction in glucose can also help to lower blood sugar levels.[110]

Emotional Pathophysiology: Unbalanced Glucose Homeostasis and Energy Due to Low Melatonin

Repeating Patterns

Doesn't complete projects. Ungrounded. Avoidance of heart feelings. Does not engage in the sweetness of life. Emotionally overreacts as protection—pancreatic, lung and heart issues. Can't cope with the emotions of others.

Emotional States

- ❖ Shortened approach to their being*. Always looking for the easy way or the shortcut to get things done. Often yields sloppy results and is an annoyance to others. Doesn't want to be bothered with life and all the hassle of being an adult. Familial/ancestral/epigenetic. Attitude of can't be bothered.

    Clarification: This person does not spend the time to be present to themselves. No energy is given to the understanding of self.

---

[110] Dragoi CM, Arsene AL, Dinu-Pirvu CE, Dumitrescu IB, Popa DE, Burcea-Dragomiroiu GTA, et al. Melatonin: A Silent Regulator of the Glucose Homeostasis [Internet]. Carbohydrate. *InTech*; 2017. Available from https://dx.doi.org/10.5772/66625

- ❖ False impressions about meaningless stuff – gives it way more value in their life than possible. Idealistic in their thoughts, they are not grounded or anchored in the knowingness of presence.

- ❖ Washed away – they were swept up in emotions with any little hiccup in their lives. A hiccup would unmoor them. They would feel unsteady and as if bad things would happen to them. Safer not to be present to the turmoil, crazy, anger and possible violence.

- ❖ Harsh conditions in their life forced them into an altered state to survive – never really present to the chaos. They would enter their own world. They had an imaginary world as a child and then as an adult. They kept unrealistic approaches to life – money issues led to more reasons to stay in the alternate view of reality.

- ❖ Sharp divisions were seen in how they would get things done. They never seemed to float into that space of completion; they would float to the next project and job. They would find themselves in jobs that had small tasks that indicated completion. They could not enter a space of largeness.

Fears

- ✦ Fear of doing anything for too long
- ✦ Fear of life
- ✦ Fear of flow
- ✦ Fear of looking inward
- ✦ Fear of connection
- ✦ Fear of feeling deeply
- ✦ Fear of dealing with the emotions of others
- ✦ Fear of parents
- ✦ Fear of family
- ✦ Fear of completing anything
- ✦ Fear of dealing with life
- ✦ Fear of being hurt
- ✦ Fear of being overwhelmed
- ✦ Fear of being in their body
- ✦ Fear of responsibility
- ✦ Fear of overwhelm

- ✦ Fear of being bothered
- ✦ Fear of bad things happening
- ✦ Fear of being grounded

Created Patterns

- My family is toxic.
- Life is overrated.
- I don't want to live.
- There's nothing about life that is good.
- If I complete something, I will be criticized.
- People are critical of everything I do.
- Completing a project will get you punished.
- I'm not worthy.
- I am good for nothing.
- I'm in control when I determine what I will do and not do.
- If I let someone tell me what to do, I will get hurt.
- I am not going to change.
- I can't be around emotional people.
- My mother/father is mean and hurtful.
- People overrun me.
- No one listens to me.
- There is no joy in my life.
- If I take responsibility, I will be judged/criticized/hurt.
- Bad things happen to me.
- I'm safe when I go somewhere else in my mind.
- If I stay small, no one will see me.
- When people are emotional, bad things happen.
- When people ask things of me, they take me out of my safety.

Function: DNA Repair

Melatonin has antioxidant and anti-inflammatory properties. These properties may help to protect cells from damage and promote DNA repair. The antioxidant activity helps protect cells from damage by free radicals. Free radicals are unstable molecules that can damage DNA. Melatonin helps to activate DNA repair enzymes, which are responsible for repairing damaged DNA. Melatonin can help to protect cells from damage by environmental toxins, such as radiation and chemicals.[111,112]

Emotional Pathophysiology: Impaired DNA Repair Due to Low Melatonin

Repeating Patterns

No foundations. Has no idea what to rely on. Unsupported. ACOA, PTSD, Dizzy spells, headaches. Confusion when confronted or even asked a direct question. They have to keep moving where they live. Digestive issues (stomach is in knots). Frequent headaches or migraines. Moves from relationship to relationship.

Emotional States

- ❖ Falsehoods were their reality. Nothing was true. Nothing was ever done. Promises are never kept. All of life was never reliable. Parent(s) lived in an alternate system of belief. Parent(s) were never present for their needs. Disappointment was punished. They kept

---

[111] Mir, SM, Aliarab, A, Goodarzi, G, et al. Melatonin: A Smart Molecule in the DNA Repair system. *Cell Biochem Funct.* 2022; 40(1): 4- 16. Available from https://onlinelibrary.wiley.com/doi/abs/10.1002/cbf.3672

[112] Liu, R., Fu, A., Hoffman, A. E., Zheng, T., & Zhu, Y. (2013). Melatonin Enhances DNA Repair Capacity Possibly by Affecting Genes Involved in DNA Damage-Responsive Pathways. *BMC Cell Biology*, *14*, 1. Available from https://doi.org/10.1186/1471-2121-14-1

their knowledge of their parent(s) lies to themselves until their lies became their identity.

- ❖ House of cards. They created a series of factors in their life that reflected a delicate balance that would come tumbling down with a slight wind of change. They created a world of false hope in their imagination. Fragile. To keep their house of cards intact, they ran away from anyone who tried to tell them they existed in a house of cards.

Fears

- ✦ Fears promises
- ✦ Fears relying on others
- ✦ Fears confrontation
- ✦ Fears vulnerability
- ✦ Fears disappointment
- ✦ Fears the truth
- ✦ Fears observations of others
- ✦ Fears judgment
- ✦ Fears of having to answer
- ✦ Fears staying still
- ✦ Fear of staying in one place
- ✦ Fear of rejection

Created Patterns

- Promises are lies
- Letting people know how you feel will get you hurt.
- When people ask me a question, I get confused.
- I can't rely on others.
- I have to move abodes.
- I can't stay in the same place for very long.
- People criticize me.
- People judge me.
- If you tell the truth, you are going to be hurt.
- If I let someone know I am disappointed, I will be blamed.
- If I stay still, they will find me and hurt me.

- Telling the truth is dangerous.
- I'm not good enough.
- I am alone.

www.ingramcontent.com/pod-product-compliance
Lightning Source LLC
Chambersburg PA
CBHW082200070526
44585CB00020B/2213